Honest Eats

Celebrating the Rich Food History of Indiana's Historic Lincoln Highway

By Keith Elchert & Laura Weston-Elchert

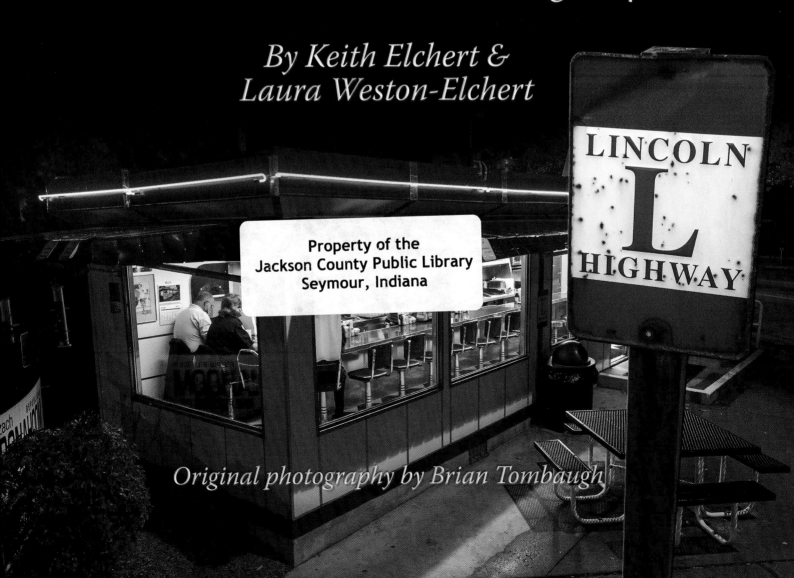

Original photography by Brian Tombaugh

Courthouses such as Whitley County's in Columbia City are a common site along Indiana's Lincoln Highway route. (Brian Tombaugh)

M.T. Publishing Company, Inc.™

P.O. Box 6802
Evansville, Indiana 47719-6802
www.mtpublishing.com

Copyright © 2016
Keith Elchert and Laura Weston-Elchert

Graphic Designer: Amanda Reyher

Library of Congress Control Number: 2016932065
ISBN: 978-1-938730-91-7

Printed in the United States of America

Foreword

This refreshing look at Indiana's historic Lincoln Highway offers great suggestions on the best places to stop along the road, but it's much more than that. As you read through this well-researched cookbook of sorts, the stories take you back in time and offer a depth of understanding about the genuine and diverse Hoosiers who have left footprints in history.

The book offers treasured family recipes, historical background and architectural highlights. The common thread linking the sites and culinary history has always been the traveler's experience — the joy of the two-lane journey.

Whether you enjoy this volume from your kitchen table or as a travel companion, you are sure to learn a great appreciation for the ethnically diverse Hoosiers who have offered food and hospitality to travelers for generations.

A number of years ago, an email from Laura led to us sharing a lunch at Club Soda in Fort Wayne. Her interest in Indiana history and knowledge of architecture was evident. She became a leader in the Indiana Lincoln Highway Association and eventually its president. Since then, Keith joined her on a culinary and writing journey that has culminated in the publishing of this extraordinary book. It is a wonderful resource for foodies and travelers along the Indiana Lincoln Highway Byway today and will serve as a historical record in the future.

Jan Shupert-Arick
Indiana Lincoln Highway Association founder and past Lincoln Highway Association president

Acknowledgements

Jan Shupert-Arick has to come first as we recognize those who helped shape our work. In addition to her support, help and encouragement, Jan deserves a special thank you; she was the inspiration for this book. We only hope we have added to all that she already has contributed to Lincoln Highway scholarship.

A book such as this is impossible without relying heavily on libraries, museums, newspapers and historical societies. Among those to whom we owe a debt of thanks are the Allen County Public Library (with its Ternet collection, as well as Lois Ternet herself); Kerry Hubbart and *The* (Fort Wayne) *News-Sentinel*; *The* (Fort Wayne) *Journal Gazette*; the (Fort Wayne) History Center, especially Walter Font; the Indiana Lincoln Highway Association board; Dani Tippmann, Jeanette Brown and the Whitley County Historical Society; the Mishawaka Public Library; the History Museum in South Bend, especially Marilyn Thompson and Kristen Madden; the LaPorte County Museum; the National Register of Historic Places; the Porter County Historical Society; the Dyer Historical Society; Susan Gochenour and the Etna Green Museum; Linda Rippy and the rest of the staff at the Marshall County Historical Society; Warsaw Community Public Library; and Noble County Public Library.

Also deserving of thanks are Rick and Leslie Monroe, Don Holterman, Bill Arick, Russell Rein, Jaclyn Goldsborough, Randy Harter, Kurt Garner, Melody Schmitt-Foreman (for her copy editing and her company in the car), Catherine Parkins, John Felger (for his research assistance), Joanne Thompson (for her extensive collection of Holter's Roost images), Deb Eidson (for research assistance), Craig Leonard (for his help in access to photographs and postcards), James Grant (for his assistance in research), Tim Harmon (for his help in securing images), Christy Keller (for cover consultation), Tina (Wolford) Tombaugh (for the loan of her husband and inspiration for the title), Joyce McCartney (for her keen proofreading eye), and our family, friends and co-workers for their support and guidance.

Finally, a huge thanks to everyone who sat for an interview with us. We hope we've captured you and your businesses accurately; any oversights or omissions are strictly on our part.

Ligonier is known for the murals throughout the town that celebrate its more than century-and-a-half heritage. A mural on Lincolnway West celebrates Ligonier's transportation history including, in the right panel, the Blazed Trail Garage and its famed big wrecker. (Brian Tombaugh)

Biographies

LAURA WESTON-ELCHERT

Laura Weston-Elchert is the multimedia editor for *The News-Sentinel* in Fort Wayne, Indiana. She is a native of Marion, Ohio, and a graduate of Westfield (Indiana) High School. She holds a bachelor's degree in American history from Ball State University and studied historic preservation and urban planning in graduate school there. She served three years on the board of the Indiana Lincoln Highway Association, including serving as president in the highway's centennial year in 2013.

KEITH ELCHERT

Keith Elchert is copy editor of the editorial pages for *The Journal Gazette* in Fort Wayne, Indiana. He is a native of Tiffin, Ohio, and a graduate of Tiffin Columbian High School. He has a bachelor's degree in communication from the University of Dayton and a master's degree in journalism from Ball State University.

BRIAN TOMBAUGH

Brian Tombaugh currently provides technical support for Apple mobile phones and computer tablets, as well as doing freelance editorial photography around Fort Wayne, Indiana. He spent 25 years as a professional newspaper photographer. He was a staff photographer at *The* (Fort Wayne) *News-Sentinel* from 1990 to 2004 before serving as the Director of Photography from 2004 to 2010. He had previously worked at *The Journal* in Lorain, Ohio, from 1984 to 1990. In 1987, he was an honorable mention for Ohio News Photographer of the Year. Brian has taught classes in beginning photography, beginning digital photography and Adobe Photoshop Elements.

Contents

1928 Southern Route

Genuine and generous.

They're words Laura first used to describe the kinds of people we'd met in our Lincoln Highway travels after we received free doughnuts (not a dozen, but two dozen) at the end of an interview with Katie Branning at New Haven Bakery. We're grateful for the pens and the refrigerator magnets, but we didn't get into this project for the free stuff we could get out of it. What we've learned has been far more valuable. We hope you'll find value – and enjoyment – in it, as well.

As journalists employed by separate newspapers in Fort Wayne, Indiana, this was our first chance to collaborate rather than compete. (Photographer Brian and Laura were co-workers for nearly 20 years and worked together on two pictorial books of Fort Wayne history.) We spent dozens of hours crisscrossing Indiana on both its northern and southern Lincoln Highway routes, often with one or both of our preteens along for the ride.

Our primary purpose was to discover the restaurants along the route – especially those that have a highway-related history or something else unique to recommend them. We were struck by the sheer variety of options available as you travel the state that bills itself as the Crossroads of America. Along the route, you'll find authentic Italian and German food in addition to the usual diner fare. Many owners and proprietors were kind enough to share with us recipes that are special to them; you'll find those recipes paired with their entries. We haven't prepared every recipe ourselves. But we did try the food pretty much everywhere we stopped, and we can promise you it's all tasty. (Our children Holly and Nicholas have developed pretty discerning palates, too. Holly got so caught up in the adventure that she even started keeping a journal of her travels.)

So many places are gone; the emerging dominance of the four-lane U.S. 30 in the 1950s and '60s corresponded with the decline and subsequent disappearance of many Lincoln Highway-dependent businesses. We've highlighted some of those as places "Out of the Past," and included recipes with some of them, as well. You'll also discover some places we've designated as "Featured Landmarks," non-restaurant stops that caught our eye. There were even a couple of occasions when a place was so unique that it drew us off the Lincoln Highway – but not too far.

A final note about our book's structure: The Lincoln Highway through Indiana follows two routes as well as any number of naming conventions, depending on where you are. The original route, which veered north toward South Bend after leaving Fort Wayne, was established in 1913. By 1928, the route had been straightened and shortened. We return to that southern route after first tracing the original route.

We're sure there are special places, both present-day and past, that we've missed. Among all those we've featured, we hope we've included your favorites. If not, let us know so our next printing can be even more comprehensive.

We also hope this book will help you find some new favorites and – above all else – more frequently take the road less traveled. There are plenty of gems waiting for you along the way, not to mention a few surprises. Two of our favorites: the time we had to stop for a pig crossing the road in Inwood, and the "suicidal cucumbers" we watched falling off a truck overloaded with pickles-to-be that we followed from a farm outside Valparaiso.

But before we start our east-to-west travels, we first need to head south for a little background.

– Keith Elchert

An early Lincoln Highway traveler, his car adorned with the highway logo, poses at the cast-iron marker at the Ohio-Indiana state line. (Courtesy Lincoln Highway Association Collection, University of Michigan)

AN IDEA IS BORN

The Athenaeum / The Rathskeller

407 E. Michigan Street
Indianapolis
(317) 636-0396

The Lincoln Highway traces its origin to Indiana. On September 10, 1912, auto dealer and Indianapolis Motor Speedway developer Carl Fisher hosted a dinner at the city's Das Deutsche Haus. That evening, he presented his idea of a transcontinental highway as a further boost to the burgeoning automobile industry.

A century later, the Athenaeum (Das Deutsche Haus was renamed during the anti-German sentiment of World War I) is a neighborhood hub in northeast Indianapolis. The building, designed by the grandfather of author and Indianapolis native Kurt Vonnegut, is home to a YMCA and a youth theater, among other organizations. It's also home to The Rathskeller; opened in 1894, it is Indianapolis' oldest restaurant.

The Rathskeller's traditional German meals begin with a soft pretzel with hot mustard instead of bread. Drinks, even the nonalcoholic ones, come in tall Pilsner glasses. The main dining room is bookended by a large, brick fireplace at one end and a heavy, wooden bar at the other.

The German Renaissance Revival Athenaeum, home to The Rathskeller restaurant, was built between 1893 and 1898. It was listed on the National Register of Historic Places in 1973 and underwent major renovations in time for its centennial. (Brian Tombaugh)

The Rathskeller's dining room features a massive wooden bar at one end of the room, decorated with all manner of beer steins, with a stone fireplace dominating the opposite wall. (Brian Tombaugh)

ie Mäßigkeit ist gut und fein
och darf sie nicht unmäßig
fein

Stammtisch

Black Forest cake, topped by its signature cherries and whipped cream, is a typical Rathskeller dessert offering. (Brian Tombaugh)

SAUERBRATEN

(courtesy of The Rathskeller)

Ingredients for Step 1

3 oz. onion
5 oz. carrot
5 oz. celery
4 oz. red currant jelly
3 oz. brown sugar
3 oz. sugar
6 oz. red wine vinegar
6 oz. red wine
4 oz. water
1¼ bay leaves
½ Tbsp. peppercorns
1¼ Tbsp. pickling spice
½ Tbsp. ginger
⅜ Tbsp. cinnamon
¾ Tbsp. nutmeg
3 ¾ pound beef roast, top round

Ingredients for Step 2

3 gingersnap crackers
6 oz. sugar
4 oz. red wine vinegar
2 oz. burgundy wine
¼ Tbsp. nutmeg
¼ tsp. white pepper
3 Tbsp. granulated onion
¼ Tbsp. cinnamon

Ingredients for gravy

Sauerbraten juice
2 gingersnaps
1 Tbsp. red currant jelly
1 Tbsp. sugar
½ tsp. Kitchen Bouquet
butter and flour

Method for Step 1

1. Combine all Step 1 ingredients, except beef, in pot and cook over high heat until mixture begins to boil. Reduce to low heat, simmer 45 minutes.
2. Allow marinade to cool, then cover and place in refrigerator for one day.
3. Clean beef roast of excess fat. Make 4-inch cross-grain cuts in beef.
4. Place in roasting pan and pour marinade over top.
5. Cover and marinate in refrigerator for 4 to 5 days.
6. Cook the meat in oven at 325 degrees for 1 ½ hours.
7. Allow meat to cool.

Method for Step 2

1. Take meat out of marinade. Reserve marinade.
2. Scrape all vegetables and spices from meat. Slice meat against the grain in 1-inch slices.
3. Place meat in new pan.
4. Strain vegetables and spices from marinade. Add Step 2 ingredients. Pour back over sliced meat.
5. Begin cooking on stovetop over high heat. Allow mixture to break a boil. Immediately reduce heat and allow to simmer until meat is very tender (about 1 ½ hours).
6. Remove meat and save marinade to make gravy.

Method for Sauerbraten Gravy

1. Combine ingredients in saucepan, bring to a boil. Add roux as needed.
2. Remove from heat.

The Rathskeller's Reuben sandwich is served with traditional German side dishes, such as German potato salad or spaetzle. (Brian Tombaugh)

The Lincoln Highway Bridge across the St. Marys River on Harrison Street carried Lincoln Highway travelers into and out of downtown Fort Wayne. The bridge plaque notes the distance to highway endpoints New York – 724 miles – and San Francisco – 2,660 miles. (Brian Tombaugh)

Allen County, the largest county along Indiana's Lincoln Highway route, has a rich and diverse food history. It's the birthplace, for instance, of the Bun candy bar. Wayne Candies made the vanilla-, maple- and caramel-flavored milk chocolate-and-peanut treats at its plant just blocks off the highway between 1906 and 1979.

Allen
COUNTY

Todd's Townley Tavern
(aka Triple Ts)

21313 East Lincoln Highway
Townley
(260) 623-6545

Todd Gremeaux has owned the building now known as Triple T's since 1998. It took a lot of work to get the place into sports bar shape, but a caved-in roof was only part of what the site has seen through the years.

Frequent Triple T's patron Jerry Love – affectionately known as the mayor of Townley – recalls tales of the 1920 Palm Sunday tornado that knocked down a grain elevator over which the restaurant is built. A 1996 recounting in The Fort Wayne *News-Sentinel* refers to the March 28, 1920, twister as northeast Indiana's worst ever; it leveled Townley, leaving 13 people dead and 34 injured. Some 150 people died that day from a series of tornadoes across the Midwest, part of a massive storm system.

By the late 1950s, the building was home to the 20th Century Luncheon, owned and run by Mattie Clauss. The Clauss family ran several restaurants in nearby Fort Wayne, and Mattie's husband had planned to run the restaurant in Townley before he was killed in a helicopter crash. Their son Stan says his mother was "renowned for her cooking ability" and developed a loyal customer base who stopped by for her doughnuts and other specialities.

Triple T's, with its wainscoted walls covered with Indianapolis Colts and NASCAR memorabilia, is a popular hangout following high school football and basketball games. Todd says his restaurant also draws "a lot of traffic from Ohio." Once there, diners can sample what Triple T's menu refers to as "great American cuisine with the comfort of home." Steaks and ribs are among the specialties, and Todd describes the atmosphere as "kid friendly." Other menu favorites include the Townley Pile Up fried appetizers basket and the Todd's Wonder Boy double hamburger.

PICKLED BEETS AND EGGS
(courtesy of Jerry and Barb Love)

6 eggs
1 can Freshlike whole small beets
¾ cup apple cider vinegar
¾ cup sugar

Boil six eggs for 10 minutes. Rinse in cold water; peel and place in 1½-quart jar. Drain one can of Freshlike whole small beets (save juice). Add beets to eggs in jar.

Bring to boil: ¾ cup saved beet juice, ¾ cup apple cider vinegar and ¾ cup sugar. Pour over beets and eggs. Place in refrigerator after a half-hour. Twist jar in refrigerator two to three times daily. Needs to be refrigerated at least three to four days before eating.

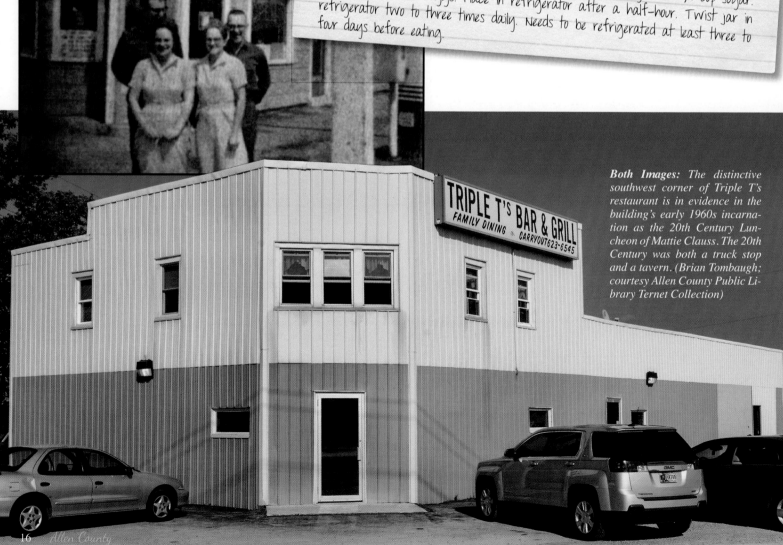

Both Images: The distinctive southwest corner of Triple T's restaurant is in evidence in the building's early 1960s incarnation as the 20th Century Luncheon of Mattie Clauss. The 20th Century was both a truck stop and a tavern. (Brian Tombaugh; courtesy Allen County Public Library Ternet Collection)

OUT OF THE PAST

Oberley's Lunch
18346 Lincoln Highway East
Zulu

A motorist along the Lincoln Highway in 1941 would have encountered this station and others like it soon after crossing the Ohio state line. "Ed and Lucy (Oberley) ran a Standard Oil station located in Zulu, Indiana, which included a small restaurant," according to a family biography in the 2005 book *History of Fort Wayne*. "Every day during the week the same customers would stop for lunch: the milkman, mailman, bus drivers, delivery drivers, etc. The place had to be marked somehow, because every hobo would stop for a free lunch. They knew they were welcome." Wednesday evenings in the summer were a special treat. "They would have free shows in the large empty lot next to the restaurant. A large outdoor screen was positioned at one end of the lot, and the projector was placed in a car, along with speakers at the other end. Everyone brought blankets and folding chairs to sit on. This all changed with the invention of television." The nearby Zulu Dance Hall was another popular recreational destination.

Also between Townley and Zulu, the present-day traveler can see what's left of what once was a Gulf gas station/restaurant that also offered cabins for rent. The area has been converted into a private residence.

(Courtesy Allen County Public Library Ternet Collection)

Billy's Downtown Zulu
18000 Lincoln Highway East
Zulu
(260) 623-3583

"Downtown Zulu" is one of those blink-and-you-miss-it intersections familiar to drivers of the original Lincoln Highway route. The tongue-in-cheek reference fits perfectly the atmosphere of a bar/restaurant where miniature statues of the Blues Brothers greet you as you enter.

Billy's has been serving winning bar food – with an emphasis on Mexican – since 1982. (The Haystack Inn preceded Billy's on the site.) Mike Adams, along with his wife, Lorie, took ownership of the restaurant in 2012. Mike is a friend of previous owner Bob Carney.

"My wife and I had many, many, many fun experiences (at Billy's)," Mike says. "We decided we didn't want to see it go down the tubes."

The Adamses also decided not to mess with a winning formula, though Mike says the restaurant (still named after the 1982 owner, Billy Nessman) was in "dire, dire need of upgrading." The inside has been completely remodeled, though Jake and Elwood retain their places of honor. The plaid pattern for the seats stayed, too. And recipes that had been set aside are in use again.

"We tried to recapture all that for customers who remember Billy's from what it was when it started," Mike says. He adds that he can tell he's onto something by the number of containers for leftovers he's going through. "The servings are plentiful, and the recipes are good," he says.

Among the popular menu choices are barbecued chicken, ribs, broiled or fried fish, and several foods featuring a Mexican twist – such as egg rolls, bruschetta and cole slaw.

Mike also has fulfilled a vision for Billy's future that included reopening on Tuesdays and the addition of a deck.

Below top: Pasta is among the specials for those looking for something other than Billy's Mexican or sandwich options. (Brian Tombaugh)

Below bottom: Though the outside looks largely the same, Billy's Downtown Zulu has undergone extensive renovations and updates since Mike Adams took over in 2012. (Brian Tombaugh)

Saint Louis Catholic Church

15535 E. Lincoln Highway
Besancon

Crossing into Indiana from Ohio on the present-day U.S. 30, the Lincoln Highway almost immediately veers off to the right. One of the first landmarks is Besancon's Saint Louis Catholic Church, with a spire that commands the landscape, even from the four-lane road to the south.

Parish literature traces the church's beginning to 1846, five years after French immigrants first arrived in the area. They dubbed their settlement "New France" as well as Besancon (after the town in northeastern France from which many of the settlers came). Other settlers made their way to Indiana from Switzerland and Germany. "Some were caught up in political persecution," says a 1996 history of the church's stained-glass windows, "while others were victims of political unrest. Many came because land was not available for them in Europe. Some just had a desire to see what was over the next hill."

A more general parish history describes how, before the establishment of the church, a priest traveled regularly from Fort Wayne, "saying Mass in the log house of Joseph Dodane." Dodanes continue to live within a mile of the church to this day. The same is true of the Lomont family; the parish history credits "Messrs. C.F. Lomont and Joseph Dodane (as bearing) the bulk of the expense of building" the original church.

Present-day parishioner Gwen Dodane counts her family as somewhat unique at Saint Louis, with "at least six generations at the church – that's a rarity," she says. "To have a family from the (founders) to now, that's rare."

The current church, listed on the National Register of Historic Places, has been in use since 1871.

"Old-timers tell us that the new church was built around the old church," says a 100-year anniversary pamphlet on the parish. "The old church was left standing within the enclosure of the new, and used for services until the new church was far enough along to be used." The original church was dismantled and carried out piece by piece once the new church was complete. The original brick façade was later covered over in a process called "sham rocking" to give the building its present stone appearance. A rectory and a school were subsequently added next door.

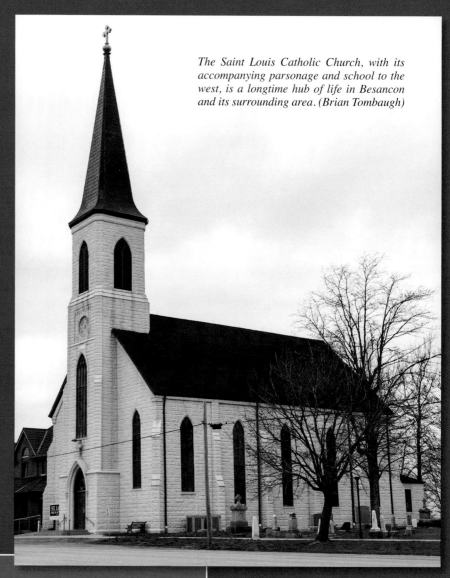

The Saint Louis Catholic Church, with its accompanying parsonage and school to the west, is a longtime hub of life in Besancon and its surrounding area. (Brian Tombaugh)

RHUBARB DESSERT
(courtesy of Gwen Dodane)

Bottom:
2 sticks butter
2 Tbsp. sugar
2 cups flour

Filling:
6 cups cut rhubarb
6 egg yolks
¼ tsp. salt
1 cup cream, milk or half-and-half
4 Tbsp. flour

Meringue:
6 egg whites
12 tsp. sugar
2 tsp. vanilla
Salt

Mix bottom ingredients, and like pie crust, pat in bottom of 9-by-13-inch pan. Bake 10 minutes at 350 degrees. Mix filling and pour into crust. Bake 40-45 minutes or until custard is set. For meringue, beat egg whites until stiff. Add sugar 2 teaspoons at a time, then vanilla and salt. Brown.

Just inside the church's main entrance is a photograph of the altar as it appeared in earlier days. That altar featured murals on the sides and an archway over the main altar with the inscription, "Come to me all you that labour, and be burdened, and I will refresh you."

Gwen remembers another feature from the past – the stretch of Lincoln Highway featuring the church had the nickname of "Gasoline Alley."

"Everybody had a little hut out front with gasoline," she says.

Gwen adds, "We grow good rhubarb along the Lincoln Highway in Indiana!"

New Haven Bakery

915 E. Lincoln Highway
New Haven
(260) 749-2161

The New Haven Bakery building has been a bakery and Lincoln Highway fixture for nearly 50 years. And for most of that time, it also has been a Branning family fixture.

Current proprietor Katie Branning took over the business from her father, a displaced International Harvester worker who bought the building after Harvester left Fort Wayne in 1983. (A previous location on the city's Main Street was destroyed by fire.) But the family tradition goes back to Katie's Uncle Fred, a baker for more than 60 years. The Brannings keep Uncle Fred's pastry cutter on hand as evidence of his love of and dedication to his craft; its blade is worn down a full inch.

The bakery remains a New Haven destination, with a steady trickle of customers from morning through early afternoon. Katie's typical day starts at 4 a.m., and the store stays open until dinnertime (when all the day's doughnuts are marked down to half price). She greets many customers on a first-name basis, and she's always grateful to see them.

"New Haven's a good town," she says. "They've been good to us."

The store is easy to spot. Just look for its hand-built neon sign. In 2004, the sign was returned to its former glory, courtesy of a Girl

New Haven Bakery's Katie Branning shares a smile with patron Mona Andrachik. The bakery is a popular place to stop in the morning for breakfast, coffee and conversation. (Brian Tombaugh)

Scout troop that had adopted the restoration as a project. "It was falling apart … really in bad shape," Katie recalls. The troop's intervention was the culmination of several previous restoration attempts, each halted by a family medical issue. "Every time we were going to work on the sign, something bad (happened)," Katie says. "I swear that sign is cursed."

Cursed or not, the sign's neon lights beckon customers to stop in for tasty treats. Among New Haven Bakery's specialties are apple fritters, cake doughnuts and cinnamon rolls; they also feature pies, doughnut holes, muffins, cookies and brownies. "We have just the basics," Katie says. "That fancy stuff just (doesn't) sell in New Haven."

Above: *Tea cookies are available by the handful as well as by the half-pound and pound at New Haven Bakery. Doughnuts and other pastries such as apple fritters also are popular. (Brian Tombaugh)*

Right: *Cakes, cookies and pastries await customers as Hope Ackerman manages the counter at New Haven Bakery. The kitchen where all the goodies are baked is in the back. (Brian Tombaugh)*

The bakery also is a go-to location for custom-baked cakes, as evidenced by the row of wedding toppers perched across the back display case. Spring is an especially busy time, with first communions, confirmations and graduations as well as the usual assortment of weddings. "By July, I'm ready for my vacation," Katie says.

Like any good baker, she has had her share of memorable cakes, such as the seven-tier number that ended up being toppled by a pair of bickering newlyweds. Then there was the customer who requested a lime-flavored cake; a box of Jell-O

APPLE CRISP
(courtesy of Katie Branning)

6 ¼ lb. apples
1 ¼ lb. sugar
⅓ cup cornstarch
1 tsp. salt
2 tsp. ground cinnamon

Topping:
6 oz. margarine
1 lb., 1 oz. brown sugar
3 oz. flour
3 oz. bread crumbs
3 oz. oatmeal
½ tsp. salt

Dice apples into 1-inch cubes. Combine cornstarch, sugar, salt and cinnamon. Add apples; mix to blend.

Cream all ingredients until well blended. Spread over apple mixture. Bake at 400 degrees for 45 minutes. Allow to cool slightly. Can be served over biscuits (see biscuits recipe). Serves 48.

BISCUITS
(courtesy of Katie Branning)

5 lb. baking flour
1 lb., 4 oz. shortening
¼ oz. salt
5 oz. baking powder
½ gallon whole milk

Mix all ingredients until well blended. Spoon onto cookie sheet. Bake in 475-degree oven until tops are brown. Makes five dozen.

mix did the trick. And Katie will finish off your cake with whipped icing if you really want it, but she recommends you stick with the buttercream.

Katie's son Kevin, who has been helping at the store since he was a teenager, seems set to carry the baking Brannings for another generation. "He's a natural," his mom says.

OUT OF THE PAST

Pagoda Inn

The Pagoda Inn, a Chinese-American restaurant operated by William Li, opened at the easternmost corner of the property dominated by Holter's Roost (see next page) in August 1954. The restaurant was a companion to one that Li owned on Lake Wawasee. A Fort Wayne *News-Sentinel* article from the grand opening describes the Pagoda Inn's "decorative pieces which have been imported from China." It adds, "The one-story restaurant … entrance leads into a lounge, beyond which lies the main dining room, which has a seating capacity of 110 persons." The article also notes that the Pagoda Inn was air-conditioned.

Less than a mile to the east sits Bell's Skating Rink, still in operation nearly 90 years after it opened in 1926. The skating rink, which many believe to be Indiana's first, was converted from a dance hall.

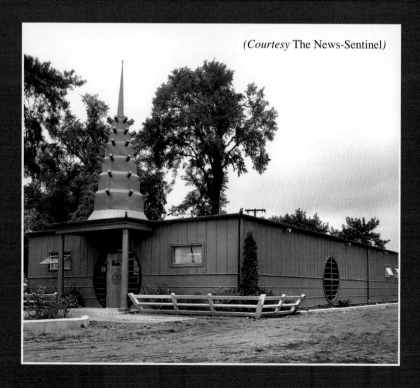

(Courtesy The News-Sentinel)

Holter's Roost
(aka The Castle)
6623 Lincoln Highway East
New Haven

In recent years, it's been everything from a real estate office to an antique store to a car dealership. It would have been an adult novelty shop were it not for the intervention of concerned neighbors. In its heyday, though, the distinctive building that many call "The Castle" was the center of a thriving chicken empire. At that time, its name was Holter's Roost.

Ruling that roost was William D. Holterman, who owned up to 50 acres along the Lincoln Highway east of Fort Wayne. A wrought-iron arch with the name "Holter's Roost" greeted visitors to the property. There, William raised chickens and packaged custom-made chicken feed that was based on a formula created by veterinarian (and congressman) William Gillie. In later years, there was enough land around the roost for Holterman to offer parcels to his two children, creating a family compound on the edge of New Haven.

The house itself was the vision of architect Henry Meyer, who was also known for his designs of churches, hospitals, schools and commercial buildings around Fort Wayne.

William Holterman's specialty was a breed of chicken known as the Aristocrat Barred Rocks (or Barred Plymouth Rocks), which was both an excellent egg-layer and a producer of tasty meat. The 1926 publication *Builders of Greater Fort Wayne* described the "hundreds of (chickens) strutting about their pens (that) excite the admiration of the many thousands of motorists who daily pass (Holterman's) house on the Lincoln Highway."

The north façade of Holter's Roost boasts the name of the home above the entrance. (Brian Tombaugh)

View of Holter's Roost that would have greeted visitors to William Holterman's home a century ago; the present-day highway runs in the background. (Brian Tombaugh)

The center spread of this 16-page brochure includes a rendering of the entire Holterman operation. All of the outbuildings have been lost as the area has been overtaken by retail and industrial development. (Brian Tombaugh)

You Are Always Welcome at HOLTER'S ROOST . . . .

Come and see all this for yourself. Yes, Come! ! Above is a partial view of Holter's Roost, the great master breeding farm where Holterman ARISTOCRATS are produced. The fame of this intensive breeding plant has spread so widely that every year hundreds of visitors from all parts of the U. S. and from foreign countries call here to see these attractive ARISTOCRATS in their home surroundings.

If you are ever near Ft. Wayne, on any day but a Sunday, be sure to call on us. We shall be happy to show you the interesting sights and most valuable birds here and personally explain the breeding program which we are carrying forward.

The beautiful home of W. D. Holterman is known far and wide in this community. You will find it 5 miles east of Ft. Wayne, facing on two paved roads, the nationally known Lincoln Highway (No. 30) and the Maumee Highway. Bus service and telephone. If you will phone us when you reach Ft. Wayne we shall be glad to give you directions how best to reach Holter's Roost.

A $100,000 Breeding Plant--devoted to the Production of Aristocrats . . .

The above photograph shows only a part of the noted breeding farm, which is the home of ARISTOCRAT Barred Rocks. Nice environment for ARISTOCRATS—isn't it? Eight more buildings and many more poultry yards could not be shown in this view. Thousands of dollars worth of the most beautiful Evergreens (such as Koster's Blue Spruce) and other elaborate landscape work (very little of which is in this view) adorn the home grounds, making it one of the delightful picturesque sights along the ocean-to-ocean Lincoln highway.

Here is every facility for the production of these world famous ARISTOCRATS—a master breeding farm where conditions are ideal.

On this intensive breeding farm we are continuously breeding and trapnesting many hundreds of fine birds in single-mated pens. From this establishment go shipments of baby chicks, of hatching eggs, of fine exhibition and production cockerels and pullets, of cock birds and record hens, and of "Holterman-mated" trios and breeding pens, bound for all parts of the world.

Right: Joanne Thompson still has one of the glossy publications that her grandfather used to promote his chicken-breeding operation. (Brian Tombaugh)

The chickens originally were just a hobby for a man who held jobs from teacher to telephone switchboard repairman, as well as bookkeeper. By 1916, though, William's hobby had so consumed his life that a profile in the journal *Poultry Success* referred to him as "one of the most talked-of poultrymen in the United States today" and cited his "world-wide reputation." The article described how he "gradually climbed the ladder of success" to attain a "home and farm, unique and picturesque in every particular, (that) is one of the show places of Ft. Wayne."

Holter's Roost saw its share of unusual occurrences, such as the 1918 gallstone operation on William's mother-in-law, 80-year-old Sophia Brudi; it took place on the kitchen table. "That in spite of all the modern and ultra modern advances in surgical science … the wielders of the scalpel and human meat saw, can still attain excellent results in the more primitive methods of carving the genus humanis, is attested by the fact that … Brudi … recently underwent an operation for a severe attack of gall stones on the kitchen table and without the use of an anaesthetic," reported *The News-Sentinel* of Fort Wayne on September 25, 1918. Sophia, who was living with her daughter and son-in-law, refused to be taken to a hospi-

HOLTERMAN'S "Aristocrats"

TRAPNESTED PEDIGREED

by America's FOREMOST BREEDER *and FANCIER of*

BARRED PLYMOUTH ROCKS

W. D. HOLTERMAN
BREEDER *and* FANCIER
FT. WAYNE, INDIANA

tal, so surgeons improvised on the spot. "The pain of the … affliction must have been so acute as to render her comparatively insensible to the pain occasioned by the surgeon's knife, for she says that she experienced practically no pain from the non-anaesthetic operation," the newspaper reported.

William and his wife, Caroline, were the parents of Louis (Lou) and Emily. Lou (who himself had his appendix removed on the kitchen table) attained regional notoriety as a baseball player; the first baseman was a charter inductee into the Fort Wayne Baseball Hall of Fame in 1961.

Lou's daughter, Joanne Thompson, has many fond memories of growing up in the shadow of Holter's Roost and numerous stories about her grandparents. For instance: "Grandma was a bootlegger." Joanne was told stories of how, during the Prohibition years, Caroline Holterman bottled beer and whiskey in the basement weekly to replace those bottles that were emptied following Lou's baseball games (in later life, Lou Holterman earned his keep as owner of Fort Wayne's Pickwick Tavern).

Joanne also recalls a red-and-white playhouse on the property, as well as two rows of stately blue spruces that came together in a point at the eastern edge of the property. "We played hide-and-seek amongst the trees all the time," she says. And living in the presence of so many chickens, she notes it was not uncommon to find a weasel or two – or a family – nesting in the back seat when getting into the car.

Joanne's brother, Don Holterman, remembers running go-carts over a 20-foot-wide creek bridge made of the same fieldstone as the house itself. The creek was directly west of the house. Among Don's other memories are the big, white chair in the living room that was exclusively his grandfather's and the banister of the curved, main staircase down which he and his sister used to slide. On the landing of that staircase was a grandfather clock that now stands watch just inside the front door of Don's rural Warsaw home.

William Holterman died July 30, 1960, at age 87. His obituary credits him as one of the founders of Indiana's Valparaiso University. William was a devout Lutheran; his father was a minister.

Several years before his death, William sold his roost of more than 40 years, whereupon The Castle began the next phase of its retail life. William's home became the property of William Li, who lived there while he operated the Pagoda Inn at the easternmost point of the property.

The restaurant is long gone, but the house survives.

A book kept by grand-daughter Joanne Thompson features Caroline Holterman's handwritten recipes. (Brian Tombaugh)

GERMAN CABBAGE
(courtesy of Joanne Thompson)

1 medium-head red cabbage
2 Tbsp. butter
2 Tbsp. brown sugar
2 Tbsp. vinegar
Pinch of salt and pepper

Cook cabbage in butter 50 minutes, then add sugar, vinegar and seasonings. Cook 10 minutes more.

STRAWBERRY BUTTER
(courtesy of Joanne Thompson)

Strawberries
Butter
Powdered sugar
Heavy cream

Mash ripe strawberries. Fold them into a hard sauce made of butter and powdered sugar and a bit of heavy cream. Serve on cake.

OUT OF THE PAST

Wolf & Dessauer
923-931 S. Calhoun Street
Fort Wayne

The glory days of the Lincoln Highway were also the glory days of a Fort Wayne landmark – the Wolf & Dessauer department store at the northeast corner of Calhoun Street and Washington Boulevard.

The store traces its origins to 1896, when Sam Wolf and Myron Dessauer partnered. Wolf & Dessauer settled into its seven-story location in 1919. According to "The Twentieth Century History of Fort Wayne": "The operation expanded over the years until the entire block from Calhoun to Clinton (Street) along Washington (Boulevard) was part of the store."

Wolf & Dessauer's most famed manager was G. Irving Latz, who bought into the company when it was incorporated in 1920. In three years, Latz moved from being a member of the ready-to-wear staff to secretary and general manager. He ran the store until his death in 1947. An obituary lauded Latz for "having an instinctive understanding of public relations toward the policies of his store, which was eminently successful under his management. He made his institution known far and wide for its vision and efficient operation."

One of the highlights of any visit to Wolf & Dessauer was lunch at the sixth-floor tearoom. A June 1921 newspaper advertisement touted the tearoom's "snowy white linen and silverware, glistening with cleanliness." The ad also promised "no annoying delays. SERVICE INSTANTANEOUS. You get just what you want and you get it immediately."

Throughout the 1940s, '50s, and '60s, Wolf & Dessauer was a downtown Fort Wayne destination for marveling at the decorations as well as shopping for Christmas gifts. (Courtesy The News-Sentinel)

Betty Stein, who worked at Wolf & Dessauer in the 1930s and '40s, recalls the tearoom as "one of the places to go and be seen."

"It was a dress-up affair," she says, with the female diners attired in hats and gloves.

An additional feature of the tearoom – which was divided into male- and female-only seating – was the women who walked through, modeling the fashions for sale elsewhere in the store. A hostess behind a desk greeted patrons as they arrived for their meal. Among the specialties on the menu crafted by tearoom manager Edith Goodyear was frozen-fruit salad. "It was to die for," Betty says. "That's what the women ordered."

The white, terra cotta building also featured a street-level soda fountain, where Betty remembers how each day she "went in and had a peanut butter-and-bacon sandwich and a cherry Coke with lots of cherries."

Wolf & Dessauer was renowned as a December destination. "It became a center for Christmas shopping and decora-tion, which attracted people in such numbers that even movement in the store was often difficult," reported *The Twentieth Century History of Fort Wayne*.

By 1940, the store's proprietors decided to broaden their holiday spirit beyond the elaborate window displays. Isabel Wilkinson Parker, of the Outdoor Advertising firm, sketched out a lighted Santa-and-reindeer display to be hung off the store's façade. The 11,000-pound, 155-foot display with its 24,717 light bulbs made its debut in a presentation to the city on November 13, 1940. At that time, it was touted as the nation's second-largest lighted outdoor sign. In 1980, after more than a decade in storage, Santa and his reindeer were repaired, reassembled and hung from the side of the Fort Wayne National Bank (now National City Bank) building. The display's annual Thanksgiving Eve lighting remains a downtown Fort Wayne holiday tradition.

Wolf & Dessauer itself, however, was a Fort Wayne tradition only until 1969. In December of that year, the store was absorbed into the L.S. Ayres chain.

EDITH GOODYEAR'S FROZEN FRUIT SALAD

(courtesy of The News-Sentinel archives and Lucinda Moody, cousin of Edith Goodyear)

⅛ cup powdered sugar
½ cup old-fashioned boiled dressing, made with juice from pineapple instead of vinegar
¼ tsp. grated lemon rind
1 cup whipped cream
½ cup Royal Anne cherries, drained and halved
½ cup Bing cherries, drained and halved
½ cup pears, drained and diced
½ cup pineapple, drained and diced
½ cup marshmallows

Mix sugar, dressing and lemon rind until sugar is dissolved. Fold in whipped cream, fruit and marshmallows. Put in mold. Freeze. Makes 8 servings or 1 quart.

EDITH GOODYEAR'S RUM PIE

(courtesy of The News-Sentinel archives and Lucinda Moody, cousin of Edith Goodyear)

Graham cracker crust:
10 squares honey graham crackers, rolled into fine crumbs
3 Tbsp. brown sugar
3 Tbsp. soft butter
1 ½ tsp. cinnamon

Mix together thoroughly. Line 9- or 10-inch glass pie pan with mixture. Bake at 350 degrees for 6 minutes. Cool thoroughly.

Rum filling:
3 egg yolks
½ cup granulated sugar
1 ½ tsp. plain Knox gelatin
¼ cup cold water
½ pint whipping cream
3 to 4 Tbsp. light rum

Beat egg yolks until thick and lemon-colored. Add sugar; beat well. Soak gelatin in small pan of water; stir and let stand until well thickened. Heat to boiling point, stirring constantly. Remove and pour into egg mixture; stir well. Let stand. Whip cream; fold three-fourths into egg mixture. Add rum and mix well from bottom of bowl. Pour into cooled pie shell. Place in freezer and chill until firm.

Topping:
2 tsp. sugar
Reserved whipped cream (from above)

Add 2 tsp. sugar to rest of whipped cream. Spread atop pie and sprinkle with grated bitter chocolate.

Cindy's Diner

230 W. Berry Street
Fort Wayne
(260) 422-1957

In January 2014, the city of Fort Wayne approved a plan to move Cindy's Diner in order to clear land for a multimillion-dollar commercial/residential development. It now sits a couple blocks northwest of its former location at 830 S. Harrison St. Though no longer on the Lincoln Highway route, the diner continues to proudly display its Lincoln Highway sign.

At Cindy's Diner, they like to say they "serve the whole world, 15 at a time." And if you're one of those 15 seated on a red-upholstered stool at the counter of the chrome diner, there's a good chance you're going to get Garbage.

"Garbage" is the signature dish whipped up on the original grill by John Scheele – or, as he often refers to himself, "Mr. Cindy." Cindy is his wife, and she can carry on a separate conversation and enjoy a slice of her husband's rhubarb pie while discussing the history of her vintage 1952 Valentine diner (Valentine, a Witchita, Kansas company, built small diners designed to be located along major highways).

"My husband bought it for me as a Mother's Day gift," Cindy says.

Above: *John and Cindy Scheele's diner has been a downtown Fort Wayne landmark for 25 years. (Brian Tombaugh)*

Left: *Doughnuts come tumbling out of the fryer at Cindy's Diner, just as they did once upon a time at G.C. Murphy's Dime Store. (Brian Tombaugh)*

And even though neither had any previous restaurant experience, the former seamstress and her building contractor spouse opened their rescued building at the corner of Wayne and Harrison streets in the fall of 1990.

Since then, they've developed a menu of breakfast and lunch favorites – patty melts and tenderloins are particularly popular. But no dish is ordered more than the one that literally came with the building.

Before Cindy's was Cindy's, it was Marge's Diner. Marge originated the Garbage dish, but John has seemingly perfected it. Cindy cautions, however, "You can't make it taste the same at home." The Scheeles know; they've tried.

Below: This plate shows Cindy's signature "Garbage" dish. (Brian Tombaugh)

The secret, she says, is the well-seasoned grill that's been a part of the diner from the start.

Another item unique to Cindy's is its doughnut machine, which was originally used at Fort Wayne's G.C. Murphy's Dime Store. The Scheeles quickly put in a claim when another diner, which at the time was home to the machine, closed. One day soon after, a man walked into Cindy's and told the Scheeles how he had put the machines together for Murphy's and had all the old recipes at home. He passed them along.

"Nobody knows how to make 'em but him," Cindy says of her husband.

The diner draws a mix of customers for its breakfast and lunch offerings, from vacationing families to businessmen in suits. Among the items they order most frequently, aside from Garbage, are Cindy's patty melts, tenderloins and milkshakes.

The nearby Embassy Theatre has led to a number of famous patrons for Cindy's. She's on her second guestbook; they bear the signatures of patrons from as far away as France and Germany, as well as all corners of the United States. Those books note visits by Doc Severinsen, Marie Osmond and members of the Beach Boys. Cindy remembers that the Beach Boys did their concert wearing Cindy's Diner T-shirts the evening after their visit.

CINDY'S DINER 'GARBAGE'

The basic ingredients are eggs, potatoes, cheese, onions and ham. Add-ins available on request include sausage, tomato, green pepper, bacon, jalapeno or habanero pepper, corned beef hash and mushrooms.

Dan Ross (foreground) and Jim Anderson share an early-morning laugh over breakfast at Cindy's, as John Scheele mans the counter. (Brian Tombaugh)

In November 1959, the Lincoln Tower was in its glory as it dominated the Fort Wayne skyline. The tower remains in use as a bank to this day. (Courtesy The News-Sentinel)

Lincoln Tower
116 E. Berry Street
Fort Wayne

Historian Michael Hawfield calls the Lincoln Tower "the very symbol of Fort Wayne's great commercial growth early in the 20th century." The 22-story art deco exemplar was Indiana's tallest building through the Lincoln Highway's glory years.

Opened in November 1930 at a cost of $1.3 million, the Lincoln Tower is built of granite, Indiana limestone and terra cotta. Its flagpole soars 312 feet above the ground, and the tower originally featured a revolving beacon.

"The seven panels depicting the various stages in the life of Abraham Lincoln constitute an interesting feature of the Berry Street entrance," notes a history provided by the Lincoln National Bank. The main lobby ceiling draws considerable attention, too; the mural by artist Glenn M. Shaw represents the energizing properties of the sun.

The original anchor tenant – Lincoln National Bank – was formed as a German-American Bank in 1905. That bank organized the Lincoln Trust Company in 1914 and itself adopted the Lincoln name on the eve of America's entry into World War I.

"It is one of the best art deco buildings in the Midwest," enthused local preservationist Angie Quinn to *The News-Sentinel*, "and it actually has one of the very best art deco interiors." Grillwork, zigzag patterns and Egyptian symbols carry the style throughout the building.

The tower underwent a $1 million restoration under new ownership in 1998.

Right: Among the wall decorations at Columbia Street West is a vintage photo of the building, dropped off years ago by someone who, Freistroffer says, thought Columbia Street should have it. The Lincoln Highway Tire Shop featured the distinctive highway "L" in its advertisement. (Brian Tombaugh)

John Freistroffer's Columbia Street West is a popular downtown Fort Wayne gathering spot. The Cajun-themed Bourbon Street Hideaway Restaurant can be found in the basement. (Brian Tombaugh)

Columbia Street West

135 W. Columbia Street
Fort Wayne
(260) 422-5055

Columbia Street traces its roots to Fort Wayne's earliest days, when it sprang up as an outpost along the Wabash and Erie Canal. Nearly two centuries later, Columbia Street West is an anchor of the city's Landing District. And in the early part of the 20th century, "the Lincoln Highway came right by our front door," the building's co-owner says.

The bar/restaurant opened in 1985, but "there's been a bar here for many, many years," says John Freistroffer (his brother Hank is the other partner). The Italianate, brick building dates to the 1830s or 1840s, John says. The present-day incarnation features a reception hall upstairs and a Cajun-and-Creole-themed bistro – Bourbon Street Hideaway – in the basement, as well as outdoor seating when the weather's appropriate. An expansion that began in 1990 nearly tripled the popular nightspot's square footage.

The atmosphere is casual; "it's not fine dining, but good," John says. Columbia Street West also hosts live bands three nights a week.

As you step out Columbia Street West's main door and glance to the left, across Harrison Street, you'll notice a pair of concrete pillars. They are all that remain of the Randall Hotel. During its Lincoln Highway-era heyday, the Randall was a five-story building that boasted 83 rooms and a 35-foot veranda across its front façade.

OUT OF THE PAST

Ye Olde Tavern
1025 Goshen Avenue
Fort Wayne

Just west of the Fort Wayne intersection known as Five Points – where the building that was once the Lincoln Highway Gas Station is now a real estate office – sits a distinctive building that once housed Ye Olde Tavern. A period postcard says the tavern offered "dancing and floor show daily." The building also has housed the A.C. Muntzinger Furniture Co. At 1012 Goshen Road sat the since-demolished Lincoln Highway Grocery.

(Keith Elchert and Laura Weston-Elchert's collection)

YE OLDE TAVERN, FORT WAYNE, IND. ST. MARY'S AVE. AT ROUTE 30 WEST. DANCING AND FLOOR SHOW DAILY.

A-917

The Venice
2242 Goshen Road
Fort Wayne
(260) 482-1618

The Venice has been serving traditional Italian favorites since 1955. When it opened in 1948, the restaurant was called the Key Dining Room and was part of a strip on the north side of the Lincoln Highway known as Key Heights; it also featured a hotel and a bowling alley (the bowling alley still stands).

Three years after the restaurant was renamed, local artist James McBride added a true Venetian touch by painting a mural along the restaurant's back wall. The mural features notable scenes of Italy's City of Canals, including its famed Rialto Bridge and St. Mark's Cathedral. An arch that separates a pair of dining areas reinforces the Venetian theme. Other decorative touches are more homespun, such as the family wedding photos and the grape-patterned tablecloths.

The food reflects that same homemade approach – at the insistence of owners Pat and Judy Finley. Doughs and breads are all prepared on site, as are tangy sauces. The buffet features entrees from pizza to baked mostaccioli to fettuccine Alfredo; mix and match to suit your taste and appetite. Lasagna is another customer favorite.

While Italian is the cuisine of choice, the Finleys (owners since 1981) enjoy mixing up the menu on occasion. The third Thursday of each month is German night. The Venice also is known for its St. Patrick's Day celebration and its Mexican–themed evenings. You can enjoy live music every Friday, and the karaoke machine gets a workout on Saturdays.

In addition to fine Italian food, you might catch a performance from an area group like the Gregg Bender Band at The Venice. (Brian Tombaugh)

"It's a really family-oriented restaurant," Judy says.

You might even catch a glimpse of one of the sports celebrities who have frequented The Venice, such as the NFL's Rod Woodson or Jason Fabini, or the NBA's Brad Miller of nearby Kendallville.

THE VENICE'S GRILLED CHICKEN BREAST CACCIATORE
(courtesy of Pat Finley)

¼ cup olive oil
3 medium onions, sliced
4 green bell peppers, sliced julienne
2 cups white mushrooms, cleaned and ¼ end
12 5-oz. boneless chicken breasts
1 large can diced tomatoes
2 Tbsp. tomato paste
1 can tomato sauce
3 Tbsp. chopped garlic
Salt and pepper to taste

Saute vegetables and place in large roasting pan. Add chicken breast, tomatoes, tomato paste, tomato sauce, garlic, salt and pepper. Roast covered in oven for 1 hour.

OUT OF THE PAST

Lincolndale Café and Dance Hall
Goshen Road
Fort Wayne

The Lincolndale is one of a cluster of Goshen Road businesses that have been lost to time and the construction of Interstate 69. The original restaurant, located on what was then Fort Wayne's western edge, was expanded to include a skating rink/dance hall, capitalizing on America's obsession with the two pastimes. A roadside stand offering Kumback (comeback) sauce – so good you'll come back for more – capitalized on the obsessions with food and Lincoln Highway travel. According to Jan Shupert-Arick in *The Lincoln Highway across Indiana*, the recipe for Kumback sauce included Thousand Island dressing, remoulade, ketchup, mayonnaise, Worcestershire sauce, mustard and pepper. The restaurant is believed to have burned in the late 1930s; the dance hall portion housed a succession of businesses before being torn down.

(Courtesy Russell Rein)

(Courtesy Russell Rein)

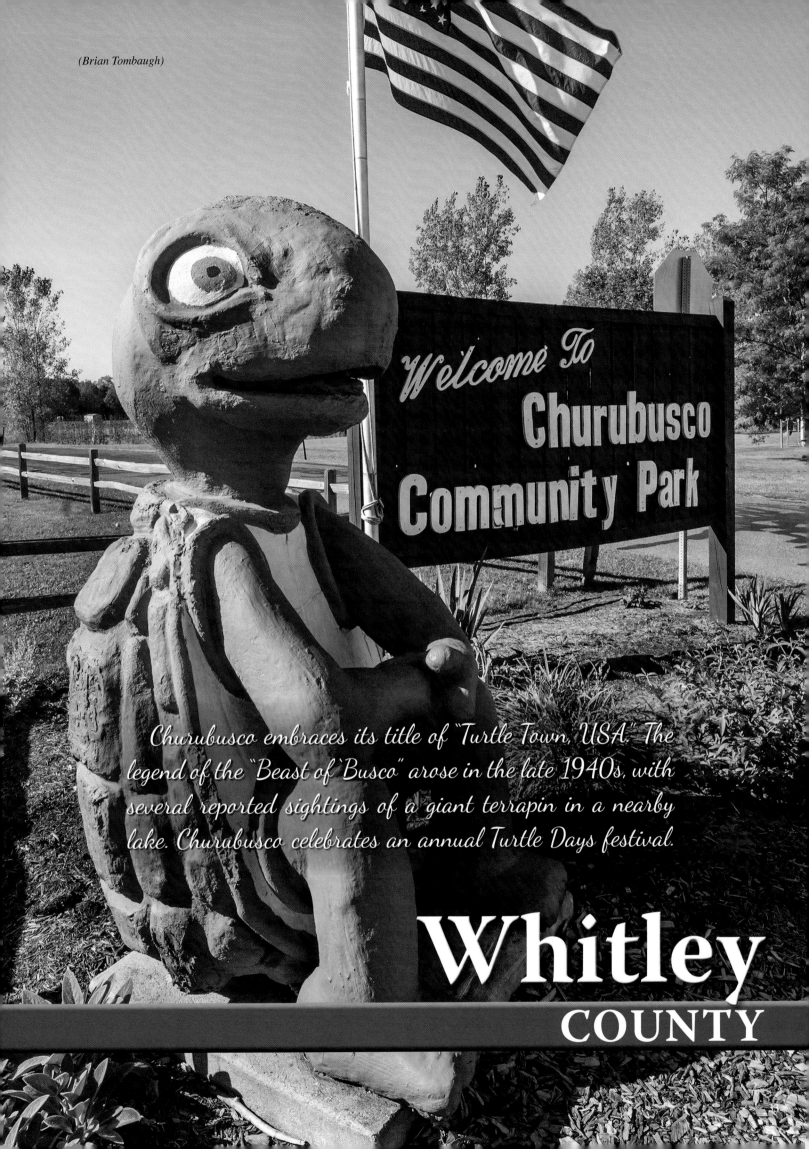

(Brian Tombaugh)

Welcome To Churubusco Community Park

Churubusco embraces its title of "Turtle Town, USA." The legend of the "Beast of `Busco" arose in the late 1940s, with several reported sightings of a giant terrapin in a nearby lake. Churubusco celebrates an annual Turtle Days festival.

Whitley
COUNTY

Magic Wand

602 S. Main Street
Churubusco
(260) 693-3518

Judy Myers and grandson David Hill keep the tradition going behind the counter at the Magic Wand. (Brian Tombaugh)

A bright, neon sign (that at one time was adorned with a Lincoln Highway marker) alongside a fairy princess and an ice cream cone beckons diners to Churubusco's Magic Wand. The landmark has long drawn highway aficionados from New York to Chicago.

The restaurant – a former Tastee Freez; the walk-up windows are still in use – started out in 1964 with five booths and a counter. These days, owners Max and Judy Myers serve up to 100 people at a time (they expanded in 1981).

Customers enjoy their double- and triple-decker Magic Burgers and breaded tenderloins surrounded by Judy's collection of clown paintings, dolls and other assorted memorabilia. The first was a gift from her mother-in-law; family, friends and customers have been contributing ever since.

Meals are frequently topped off with a dessert portion of pie (lemon meringue and coconut are among the best-sellers) or cobbler (peach, cherry, apple or Black Forest), if not one of the many ice cream treats. Another popular dessert option is the doughnuts, which are fried fresh as you finish your meal.

The family-run business is set to continue for another generation; the Myers' grandson David Hill, who earned his business management degree from IPFW, has been groomed since age 17.

MAGIC SUNDAE

(courtesy of Judy Myers and David Hill)

Fry an 8-inch tortilla shell into a bowl shape; dust with cinnamon sugar. Fill with ice cream, hot fudge, whipped cream, nuts and a cherry.

Neon lights on the outside, and clowns on the inside: All these elements – not to mention the burger – put the magic in Churubusco's Magic Wand. (Brian Tombaugh)

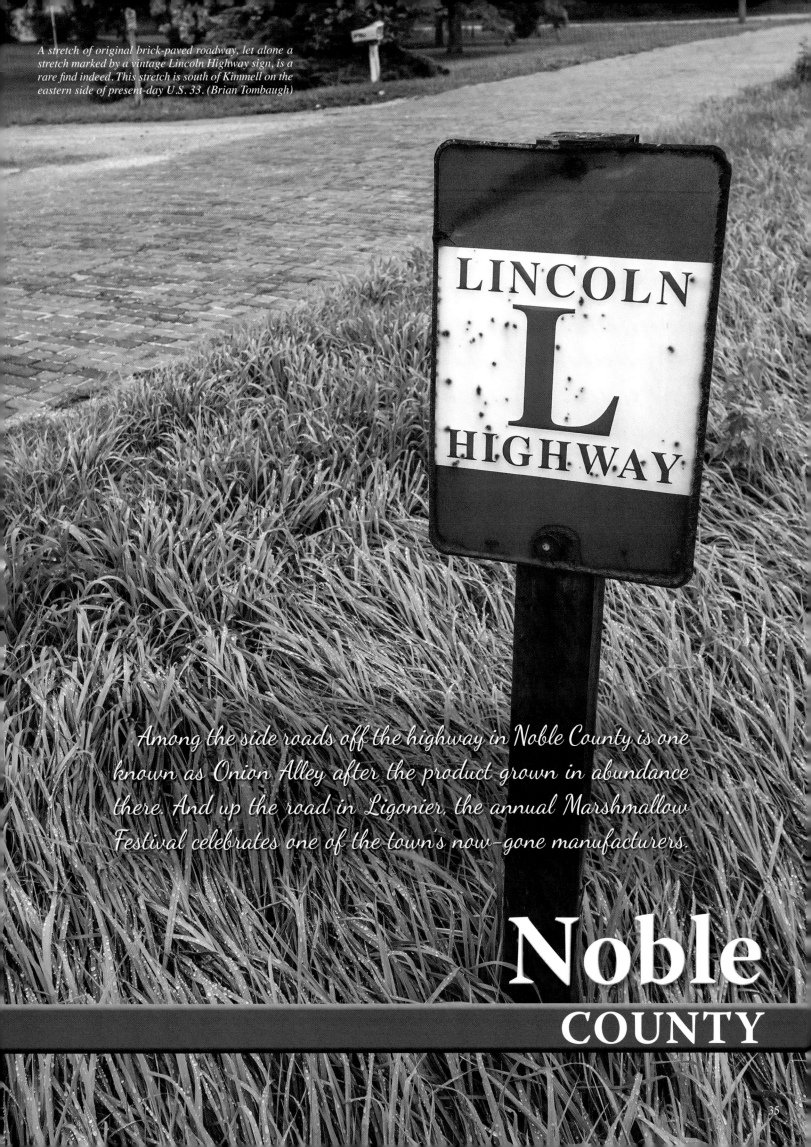

A stretch of original brick-paved roadway, let alone a stretch marked by a vintage Lincoln Highway sign, is a rare find indeed. This stretch is south of Kimmell on the eastern side of present-day U.S. 33. (Brian Tombaugh)

LINCOLN L HIGHWAY

Among the side roads off the highway in Noble County is one known as Onion Alley after the product grown in abundance there. And up the road in Ligonier, the annual Marshmallow Festival celebrates one of the town's now-gone manufacturers.

Noble
COUNTY

Luckey Hospital Museum
corner of U.S. 33 and Indiana 109
Wolf Lake
(260) 635-2490 or (260) 636-2312

Shirley Hile was born in the building that now houses the Luckey Hospital Museum. Her pride in the landmark is evident as she leads visitors on tours; schoolchildren even get to see her in a period-appropriate uniform. The building functioned as a hospital for less than 30 years, but thanks to Shirley's hobby of collecting medical artifacts (she's a retired nurse and self-confessed packrat), the museum tells a story that covers a much longer period of time.

The hospital was the brainchild of Shirley's great-uncle, Dr. James E. Luckey, who had practiced medicine from his Victorian home (long since demolished) in front of the present-day modest brick building beginning in 1902. The design of the hospital primarily was handled by James' son Harold, an electrical engineer with knowledge of construction's technical intricacies. (Harold later obtained a medical degree, as did his brother Robert. Both practiced with their father in the hospital.)

Dr. James E. Luckey is seen in a photograph in the museum room that served as his office. (Brian Tombaugh)

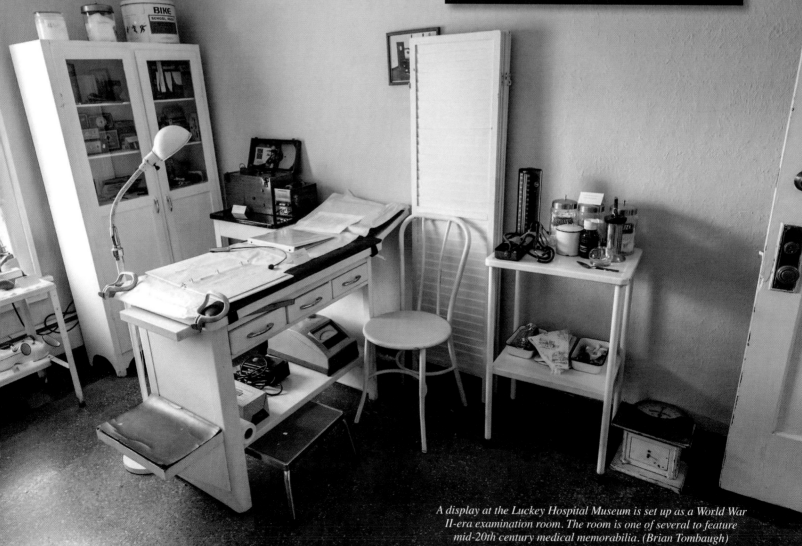

A display at the Luckey Hospital Museum is set up as a World War II-era examination room. The room is one of several to feature mid-20th century medical memorabilia. (Brian Tombaugh)

Construction began in 1929; the hospital was fully operational in 1931. A 1932 Wolf Lake history describes the "$100,000 brick hospital (as) doing a heavy business in both surgery and medicine. ... It is the most modern equipped hospital in the world." Among its 1930s state-of-the-art amenities were an oxygen tent, a nurse-call system and fire equipment. The hospital's reputation was such that surgeons from Fort Wayne would travel to practice in the building.

The hospital closed in 1957. The building then served as a nursing home, an apartment house and a private residence until Shirley and Mary Goodrich joined to buy the building in 2000. Along with Shirley's memorabilia, donated artifacts make up the collection that visitors see. The museum features a surgery room outfitted with period-specific equipment, a collection of nurse's uniforms and caps, a patient's room and a still-functioning iron lung.

HICKORY NUT CAKE
(courtesy of Shirley Hile)

Shirley says: "The recipe ...is from my grandmother, a sister to James E. Luckey (Mary Jane Luckey Starkey). ... First line of business ... was to gather the hickory nuts, shell and pick them out, about a cup. The woods on the farm where she lived ... is full of hickory trees, so it was not a problem to obtain the main ingredient. ...She used a 'Lady Baltimore' cake recipe, which is as follows."

Cake:
1½ cups white sugar
½ cup butter
¾ cup sweet milk
1 tsp. vanilla
1 Tbsp. baking powder
2 cups sifted cake flour
½ tsp. salt
4 egg whites (beaten stiff)

Begin by combining the sugar and butter and creaming. Add rest of ingredients except egg whites, then fold beaten egg whites into mixture and divide into three greased cake pans; bake at 350 degrees.

Filling:
1 cup sugar
1 Tbsp. flour
2 large eggs
1 cup light cream
¼ tsp. salt
1 cup hickory nuts
1 tsp. vanilla

Mix all ingredients. Cook until thickened on low to medium fire. Cool and spread on top and between three layers. Whatever is left over can be put on the sides (but seldom was there enough).

Another room in the museum features a display of nurses' caps, part of the display on the evolution on medical uniforms through the years. (Brian Tombaugh)

James Luckey also holds a place in Indiana Lincoln Highway lore. A good-roads proponent, James was "very, very instrumental in making sure the highway went through Wolf Lake," Shirley says. After the highway's construction, James served as Lincoln Highway consul for the Merriam-to-Ligonier stretch. The section received significant improvements through his efforts.

APPLE WALNUT CAKE
(courtesy of Shirley Hile)

2 eggs	2 cups flour
2 cups sugar	1 tsp. cinnamon
4 cups chopped apples	2 tsp. baking soda
1 cup walnuts	¾ tsp. salt
1 tsp. vanilla	½ cup oil

Mix eggs and sugar. Add chopped apples, walnuts and vanilla. Set aside. In a separate bowl, mix flour, cinnamon, soda and salt.

Mix the contents of the two bowls together. Add oil and mix until blended. Bake in Bundt pan at 350 degrees for about 50 minutes or until a toothpick comes out clean when inserted to test doneness.

JR's Dari Sweet
1066 U.S. 33
Wolf Lake
(260) 635-2045

In 2013, Kevin and Sheryl Schieferstein celebrated their 30th year running JR's Dari Sweet in Wolf Lake. The building went up in the 1950s (it's always been an ice cream shop).

Right: (Brian Tombaugh)

OUT OF THE PAST

Johnson's Strawberry Farm
2283 S. U.S. 33
Albion

For 71 of her first 75 years, Sue Johnson lived along the Lincoln Highway, and she sold produce by the side of the road for almost as long. In 2014, she finally gave in to retirement and auctioned off the assets of Johnson's Strawberry Farm. But she has a lifetime of memories to share.

Strawberries have been good to Sue Johnson throughout her life. Here she shows off a handful of the fruit that was grown in her fields just off the Lincoln Highway near Albion. (Brian Tombaugh)

Her father had given Sue her first strawberry patch at age 8 or 9, and she remembers tallying the sales she made on a cash register that Santa Claus had given her. "I was hiring help when I was 11," she says.

Sue's operation – a you-pick farm as well as a roadside stand started in 1966 – grew to require even more management. Sue vigilantly monitored her business, inspecting the fields and the chickens' roost in a golf cart dubbed "Sue's Strawberry Surrey," complete with a red fringe on top. Strawberries accounted for seven acres of her land; homegrown sweet corn and blueberries were available in season, as well.

Sue also proudly showed visitors her strawberry-themed collection, which occupied a large bedroom in her home (painted blue, not red) behind the roadside stand. The sights included strawberry-decorated clothing, curtains, pillows and wall hangings, plus nearly every sort of knickknack imaginable. Family and friends have given her strawberry collectibles from at least 27 countries around the world. The collection is actually Sue's second; the original was lost to a fire in 1983. "Everything has a story," she says. "The stories are what make it so nice."

The Lincoln Highway has played nearly as central a role in Sue's life as strawberries have. As a child, she and her brothers used to sleep on the concrete porch just a few feet from the highway when their tin-roof home was too hot on summer nights. She also used to herd cows across the highway to pasture in the morning and back home again at night. "It used to be, if somebody was coming, you'd just hold up your hand," she says.

Among Sue's fondest memories are when the highway would occasionally ice over during the winter time. Her dad would strap on his skates, she'd get out her sled, and the Lincoln Highway would be her personal playground all the way to Wolf Lake.

STRAWBERRY SHORTCAKE

(courtesy of Sue Johnson / Johnson's Strawberry Cookbook)

1 egg	3 tsp. baking powder
1 cup sugar	2 cups flour
2 Tbsp. shortening	½ tsp. vanilla
½ tsp. salt	3 cups strawberries
1 cup milk	¾ cup sugar

Cream the egg, 1 cup sugar and shortening together. Add salt and milk. Mix baking powder and flour in a separate bowl. Mix flour mixture with egg mixture, and add vanilla. Bake in waffle mold or shallow pan at 350 degrees. Cool. Mix strawberries and ¾ cup sugar. Pour over cake.

Above & below: The roadside stand in the front yard of Sue Johnson's house invited highway travelers to stop and shop for a wide variety of fresh fruits and vegetables. One note paid tribute to those customers as "the most loyal, honest, nice, etc. in Indiana!" (Brian Tombaugh)

Kimmell House Inn

1397 N. U.S. 33
Kimmell
(260) 635-2193

A visit to the Kimmell House Inn is a step back in time to a more genteel era of dining. A tidbit tray filled with finger sandwiches and sweets, all topped with a Hershey's Kisses chocolate, awaits, as does a large selection of teas. You enjoy it all in the similarly genteel atmosphere of a meticulously restored Italianate house.

The home was built in 1876 by Orlando Kimmell, an Indiana state representative as well as the farmer of more than 1,000 acres surrounding the home. He was considered so significant to the area that the nearby village of Sparta was renamed Kimmell in his honor.

"(The inn) was very livable when we bought it, but it was in need of a lot of work, too," says Dean Stoops, who owns the Kimmell House Inn with his wife, Deb. "We pretty much went through the whole inside."

Orlando Kimmell's statehouse portrait hangs in the dining room of his namesake inn. (Brian Tombaugh)

OATMEAL CAKE

(courtesy of Dean and Deb Stoops)

1 cup quick oats
1¼ cups boiling water
2 eggs
½ cup shortening
1 cup white sugar
1 cup brown sugar
½ tsp. salt
1 tsp. vanilla
1 tsp. baking soda
1½ tsp. cinnamon
1½ cups flour

Frosting:
6 Tbsp. melted butter
½ cup brown sugar
¼ cup cream
1 cup coconut
1 cup pecans

Mix quick oats in boiling water and let stand. Cream together eggs, shortening, white sugar and brown sugar. Add salt, vanilla, baking soda, cinnamon and flour. Add oatmeal mixture and mix well. Bake 25-30 minutes at 350 degrees in greased 9-by-13 pan.

Mix ingredients for frosting. Pour over warm cake.

Ornate chandeliers, wallpaper and moldings – as well as seats near the fireplace – contribute to the Kimmell House Inn's late 19th century charm. (Brian Tombaugh)

KIMMELL HOUSE INN BANANA BREAD

(courtesy of Dean and Deb Stoops)

Blend together:
- ¾ cup butter-flavored Crisco
- 2 eggs
- 1½ cups sugar
- 1 tsp. vanilla

Add:
- 1½ cups mashed, ripe bananas
- 1 tsp. salt
- 1 tsp. soda
- (Can add nuts or blueberries)

Stir in 2 cups flour; alternate with ½ cup buttermilk. Bake in two greased pans at 350 degrees for 45 minutes or until golden brown.

Both images: *A popular high tea option at the Kimmell House Inn is the tidbit tray; its three layers are filled with "three gourmet finger sandwiches, two desserts, buttermilk scones with clotted cream and fresh fruit." (Brian Tombaugh)*

They restored such touches as the dining room's tin ceiling, which was repurposed from an 1861 church and required 36 cans of spray paint to cover. And they added touches of their own such as a coffee bar, which is fronted by the legs and keyboard of a sheared-off square grand piano. The sumptuous, high-windowed dining room and parlor beckon patrons to linger. There, they can enjoy the richly detailed wallpaper and the glass grape-draped chandelier. Depending on the season, the fireplaces or the porch prove equally inviting.

The Stoopses opened the Kimmell House in 2003 as a bed and breakfast with three guest rooms plus a converted summer kitchen cottage; they have since added the restaurant. The house also has hosted several weddings and at least one family's Thanksgiving dinner.

"We've had a fair amount of business from being on the (Lincoln Highway)," Dean says. "It's a neat old house that has historical value. We're doing what we're doing so we can share it."

Thanks to preservation efforts in the 1960s, this 1839 tavern stands today as a centerpiece of the Stone's Trace property. (Brian Tombaugh)

LEMON ICE

(courtesy of Stone's Trace Historical Society board member Janet Sweeney)

4 cups water
2 cups sugar
¾ cup lemon juice

Make a syrup by boiling water and sugar together for 20 minutes. Add lemon juice and stir. Cool and strain mixture through a cheesecloth (could use a coffee filter). Pour in freezer-proof dish and freeze until solid. Serves 6–8.

original source: Boston Cooking School Cook Book, 1896

Stone's Trace
U.S. 33 and Indiana 5
Ligonier
(260) 856-2666

Roughly halfway between Fort Wayne and Goshen sits Stone's Trace, a site featuring both an 1839 Federal-style clapboard tavern and a circa-1875 brick Italianate home. The Pioneer Festival that has taken place there each September since 1974 celebrates the legacy of Noble County's earliest settlers.

The location's namesake, Richard Stone, laid claim to the strategic site in 1835. He arrived from Fort Wayne in 1829, having followed a path blazed in 1790 by Gen. Anthony Wayne himself as Wayne and his troops widened an old Miami Indian trail.

Richard opened his tavern in 1839, and the building served multiple functions for the growing community. Most notably, Stone's Trace was the venue where nine horse thieves were convicted at the conclusion of a 10-day trial. In addition to a courtroom, the tavern also served as a post office, a jail and a school. The building was moved several hundred feet sometime after the property was bought by the Kimmell family in 1860; the Kimmells also were responsible for adding the brick home on the three-acre site. During this era, the tavern fell into steady disrepair as it was used to store farm feed and equipment.

New life was breathed into the building thanks to the efforts of Ligonier pharmacist Graydon Blue and his wife, Helen. In 1964, Graydon marshaled the resources of community volunteers to restore the tavern to its 1840s glory, using nothing but donated materials. Among the finds of the restoration, according to an article in *The (Fort Wayne) Journal Gazette*, was "a benchlike structure (that was) carefully put aside for investigation. Examination disclosed it had been the old bar of the tavern, and even the change drawer was intact." The same article described how "Eli Lilly, famous Indianapolis pharmaceutical manufacturer, heard of this historical flurry in Ligonier and made a special trip to Blue's pharmacy. After a 2-hour visit, he wrote a $1,000 check to endow the project."

Today, Stone's Trace continues its mission "to give the past a future" by hosting twice-yearly hearthside dinners in addition to the Pioneer Festival. An authentic 19th century, eight-course meal is served each May and October by Stone family re-enactors who also share period music and stories. Diners are welcome to dress in period costumes, as well.

Solomon Mier Manor Bed & Breakfast

508 S. Cavin Street
Ligonier
(260) 894-3668

The proprietors of the Solomon Mier Manor Bed & Breakfast invite their patrons to "enjoy a step back in time." Specifically, back to 1899, when local banker and carriage builder Solomon Mier moved into the Queen Anne-style home.

Opposite page: A 1905 Seth Thomas clock stands in Triangle Park outside the Mier House. The clock was a gift to the city in 1924 from John Cavin, son of Ligonier's founder. It stood downtown until it was severely damaged when hit by a truck in 1981. After 18 months of painstaking renovations by a Massachusetts specialist, the clock, a symbol of the town, was installed at its present site in December 1984. (Brian Tombaugh)

The home's four guest rooms – each with its own bath, flat-screen television and wireless Internet access – can accommodate up to 12 guests an evening. Guests from as far away as Germany and South Africa have spent the night at the manor. The home also has hosted luncheons, showers, dinners and even the occasional small wedding.

The Solomon Mier House Bed & Breakfast occupies a place of prominence south of downtown Ligonier, much as it did when it debuted in 1899 as home to one of the town's most notable residents. (Brian Tombaugh)

Solomon (who was Jewish) and his wife spent about their final decade in the home. It is currently owned by Amanda and Tom Smith, who run the bed-and-breakfast and have their own residence in the basement (where they've tried, without luck, to confirm the rumors of tunnels to other nearby homes). When the house came up for auction, Amanda toured it with her parents and fell in love with it. "For as old as it is, it's been very well kept," she says.

The first floor has been preserved in all its late-Victorian-era elegance. That includes a dining room with hand-painted canvas murals on the ceiling and a built-in, dark-wood buffet. The Smiths have done their best to maintain historical accuracy, but "it would be really neat to know what it looked like when it was originally done," Amanda says. Also on the first floor are a music room with a player piano (and at least 50 piano rolls) and two kitchens – one kosher.

CHOCOLATE CHIP SCONES

(courtesy of Amanda Smith)

1 cup sour cream or buttermilk
1 tsp. baking soda
4 cups flour
1 cup sugar
2 tsp. baking powder
¼ tsp. cream of tartar
1 tsp. salt
1 cup butter
1 cup milk chocolate chips
1 egg, beaten
1 Tbsp. vanilla
Garnish: sugar

Stir together the sour cream or buttermilk with the baking soda and set aside. Combine flour, sugar, baking powder, tartar and salt, then cut in butter and add chocolate chips. To the sour cream/buttermilk mixture, add the egg and vanilla. Combine with dry ingredients just until moistened. Turn dough onto lightly floured surface; use scone pan, or roll out into two half-inch-thick pats of dough and cut into wedges. Place on baking sheet, sprinkle with sugar, and bake at 350 degrees for 12-15 minutes.

The staircase leading to the second floor is illuminated by a bronze-statue lamp and a large bay window. The window is a replacement for a stained-glass depiction of the biblical matriarch Rebekah that was sold (as was the original dining room chandelier) by a previous owner in the 1970s. The carriage house also has long since been lost ("We don't know what happened to that," Amanda says), but a carriage much like the one that first brought the Mier name and house to prominence is on display at the side of the mansion.

Fashion Farm

**1680 Lincolnway West
Ligonier
(260) 894-4498**

Fashion Farm proprietors Russell and Patty Becker are working hard to keep their business moving forward – but always with an eye toward the past.

"We're not sitting back and doing nothing," Russell says in describing the farm's far-flung enterprises. "We're still dreaming a little bit."

October, normally the busiest month of the year on any farm, holds an even more special place at Fashion Farm. The tradition dates back a generation to Patty's father, Charles Williams, who became known as "Charlie Pumpkin" after he started the farm's annual Pumpkin Fantasyland in 1972. (Charles also gave the site its name; Ole Fashion was the first 4-H calf he purchased.) Among the highlights that draw roughly 30,000 people annually are the pumpkins decorated by a local artist in the likenesses of all the U.S. presidents. Characters from stories and movies also are created from gourds and squash as well as pumpkins.

Above: *A room at This Ole House Memories is reserved for telling the life story of Fashion Farm founder Charles Williams, aka "Charlie Pumpkin." (Brian Tombaugh)*

Left: *Patty Becker shows off one of the greenhouses that are part of the growing Fashion Farm business just outside Ligonier. (Brian Tombaugh)*

Fashion Farm is a restaurant, too. During the month of Fantasyland, pumpkin cookies and ice cream are added to the menu. Pumpkin doughnuts are another October favorite. Patty says they sell nearly 15,000 in the 31 days they're available.

The restaurant, which can seat 100 people and has a private dining room that can host up to 30, also was part of the vision of Charlie Pumpkin. It grew from his original idea of an ice cream shop. The restaurant has featured the cooking of head chef Marie Dillon since its opening in 1975. Russell describes Fashion Farm's menu as "mom-and-pop kind of hot-plate lunches," adding that "we make all of our own salads … pies and … ice cream." Breakfast and dinner are served, as well.

A portion of the restaurant showcases original farm-building construction; a former granary sturdily encased by poplar boards is now the private dining room.

The expanding Fashion Farm operation also features a greenhouse and a landscaping business run by the Beckers' son. In the greenhouse/garden center – which is decorated with vintage farm implements – you can get onion sets, fertilizer or yard decorations.

"We're one of the very few places in the area that does bulk seed anymore," Patty says while showing off a wall of seed bins. Another of the greenhouse's specialties is "people pots" – plantings that are customized for families.

The Countryscapes and Gardens landscaping business handles community-space plantings for surrounding towns including Columbia City, Syracuse and Ligonier.

Also on the property of the still-functioning, 200-acre family farm (which through the years has turned out produce, cattle, pigs and chickens) is This Ole House Memories. The house is Patty's childhood home, turned into a museum showcasing the memorabilia of six generations, all lovingly preserved and labeled.

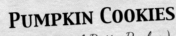

PUMPKIN COOKIES

(courtesy of Patty Becker)

1 cup shortening
1 cup white sugar
1 egg
1 cup canned pumpkin
2 cups flour
1 tsp. baking soda
1 tsp. baking powder
1 tsp. cinnamon
¼ tsp. ginger
Dash of salt

Icing:
3 Tbsp. butter
4 Tbsp. milk
½ cup brown sugar
1 cup powdered sugar

Mix shortening, sugar and egg until light. Add pumpkin. Mix well. Add flour, baking soda, baking powder, cinnamon, ginger and salt. Mix well. Dough will be a little stiff. Drop onto cookie sheet and bake 10-12 minutes in 350-degree oven. Let cool.

Heat butter, milk and brown sugar, stirring constantly to rolling boil. Stir in powdered sugar. Frost cookies while warm.

Below: *Colorfully labeled drawers and jars help employees sort the wide variety of seeds for sale at the Countryscape Floral & Gifts area of the Fashion Farm complex. (Brian Tombaugh)*

GOSHEN
HISTORICAL
SOCIETY

A fortresslike, concrete-block police booth capped by a steel turret with seven gun-portal-equipped, bulletproof windows sits outside the Elkhart County Courthouse in downtown Goshen. Attached is this historical marker: "Erected 1939 to protect the Maple City from gangsters who might travel along this the old transcontinental Lincoln Highway." The booth became the police's point of contact with the public; it was manned 24 hours a day until about 1970.

Elkhart
COUNTY

The Electric Brew
118 E. Washington Street
Goshen
(574) 533-5990

This interview took place in The Electric Brew's original location at 136 S. Main St. In the summer of 2013, the coffeehouse moved around the corner.

The Electric Brew owner Myron Bontrager describes his business as a "community gathering place." It's the kind of place that welcomes college students and senior citizens to linger over coffee and a cinnamon roll with their laptop or the newspaper amid the hum of conversation on even the dreariest of Saturday mornings. The kind of place where the smell of coffee beckons you from the sidewalk as you approach.

Below: Myron Bontrager, coffee cup in hand, poses at the original Electric Brew location on Main Street with some of the sweets from the kitchen. (Brian Tombaugh)

Above: Bald Brothers is the house blend at The Electric Brew; it's one of more than a dozen coffees available. (Brian Tombaugh)

The current location at 118 E. Washington St. touts The Electric Brew as "Goshen's Original Coffee House," with "every bean roasted here." (Brian Tombaugh)

Myron – a minister – has owned The Electric Brew since 2007. He bought Goshen's original coffeehouse from its founder, a Goshen College graduate who was a native of Oregon. "(The Electric Brew) has had a West Coast influence from the very beginning (in 1996)," he says. Family plays a big role in the Brew, as well; his sons (who are co-owners) roast coffee beans, and his daughters-in-law also help out.

As for The Electric Brew's food and drink, Myron says: "If it can be done here, we do it here." Employees make their own yogurt and salad dressings, as well as those "killer" cinnamon rolls, as Myron describes them. Bald Brothers Blend is the house brew.

The Electric Brew helped spur Myron's interest in downtown Goshen revitalization. He was a leader of the Face of the City movement that evolved into Downtown Goshen Inc. The coffeehouse also has been active in the city's First Friday events, which have drawn up to 5,000 visitors downtown.

BLUEBERRY TEA CAKE
(courtesy of Myron Bontrager)

Ingredients:
2 eggs
1½ cups sugar
½ cup butter, melted
4 cups flour
1 tsp. salt
1 cup milk
3 cups blueberries

Topping:
1 cup sugar
½ cup flour
1 tsp. cinnamon
½ cup butter, melted

Combine all ingredients and pour into dish. Mix topping and sprinkle on top. Bake for 25 minutes at 375 degrees or 50-55 minutes at 300 degrees.

Mattern's Butcher Shop & Corner Deli
201 S. Main Street
Goshen
(574) 971-8906

Dustin Mattern carries on the tradition of his grandfather, who opened a wholesale meat plant in 1954. Today, Dustin co-owns a meat market and deli with his father. But the Purdue University graduate's background is in horticulture. In 2007, he returned to Goshen from Chicago, intent on making a career change.

Bill and Dustin Mattern's deli is a popular downtown Goshen lunch spot with a wide array of sandwich choices. (Brian Tombaugh)

"People always need food; they don't always need landscaping," he says.

What began as a stand at the Elkhart Farmers Market has grown into a store dominated by a 44-foot meat counter – "the biggest … in the county," Dustin says. A well-worn wooden floor is testament to the building's durability, if not its former purpose. For 125 years, what is now Mattern's was Newell's, a women's dress shop. A stained-glass window with the store name was kept during the building's conversion. A number of pieces from the store also were repurposed; a former jewelry case now holds baked goods.

Dustin Mattern is mindful of the importance of shopping locally (for him, within a 150-mile radius of Goshen). His meat shop stocks locally raised chicken, Indiana pork and Midwest beef. The turkeys are Amish-raised and are a particular holiday favorite; sales have doubled every year. And the seafood arrives weekly from Chicago. Dustin makes that trip himself.

The deli portion of the business was added in 2009. "Not too many people are crazy enough to start a business in the middle of a recession," he says. "The whole lunch thing was an afterthought; it was a good afterthought." The menu features 20 to 25 sandwiches (plus a create-your-own option) and salads. Both indoor and outdoor seating are available.

MATTERN'S PULLED PORK SANDWICH

(courtesy of Dustin and Bill Mattern)

1 cup salt
1 cup brown sugar
¼ cup pepper
¼ cup garlic powder
8 lb. fresh pork shoulder roast
1 fresh head of green cabbage
1 bottle apple balsamic vinegar (Olive Branch)
10 sweet rolls (large for sandwiches)

To prepare rub and pork shoulder: Mix salt, brown sugar, pepper and garlic powder together. Rub generously over the fresh pork shoulder. Smoke for 4-6 hours at 225 degrees. Let cool for 6-8 hours in refrigerator. Then place in a roasting pan and roast the pork shoulder in oven for 4 hours at 325 degrees, until pork shoulder falls apart with a spoon. Pull apart.

To prepare sandwiches: Shred green cabbage and toss in the apple balsamic vinegar. Place a generous portion of pulled pork on the bottom half of the roll. Then place a big tong-full of cabbage and vinegar mix over the pork. Lastly, pour additional amount of apple balsamic vinegar over the pork and cabbage, and put a slab of your favorite cheese on the sandwich. Put the top of the roll on and dig in!

Makes 10 large sandwiches

Below: The stained-glass window that advertised Newell's dress shop now welcomes customers to Mattern's Butcher Shop & Corner Deli. (Brian Tombaugh)

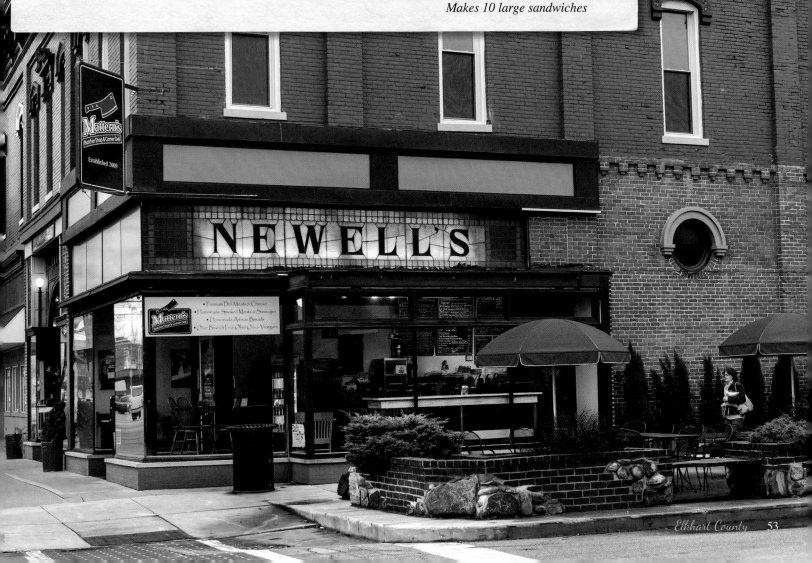

Olympia Candy Kitchen

136 N. Main Street
Goshen
(574) 534-6345

Olympia Candy Kitchen has been around a year longer than the highway that passes by its front door. In 1912, Nicholas Paflas, a Greek immigrant who his great-grandson says "just jumped off the train in Goshen," began making hand-dipped chocolates and running the soda fountain. Four generations later, the Paflas/Andersen family carries on the tradition, with each generation making its own contribution. (As of 2012, Nicholas' son, then 89, still worked three days a week making the potato salad.)

Whether the lunch counter (which became a fixture in 1920) or the candy is the bigger draw depends on the season, says current proprietor Kare Andersen, Nicholas' great-grandson. Candy is the main attraction from Christmas through Easter; along with Valentine's Day, Kare refers to the holidays as "the big three." Through the summer, the soda fountain and sandwiches keep Olympia busy.

"Half of our customers are regulars," Kare says of the lunchtime crowd. "It's kinda like 'Cheers' – we even have a 'Norm.'"

The Elkhart County Courthouse across the street provides a source of customers, as well. Kare tries to keep the conversation among the attorneys, jurors and regulars light.

"I always tell 'em: No religion or politics," he says. Perhaps that's another reason Olympia bills itself as "the sweetest little place in town."

Across from the counter, where patrons perch on red vinyl-covered stools, Olympia's candy is displayed in massive glass-paneled, wooden cases originally imported from Europe. The dining area to the back of the store is framed by mirrors and features dark, wood-paneled booths with Formica tops. Both there and at the counter, customers enjoy food featuring Olympia's chili and mayonnaise, each homemade, as well as sodas made from Olympia's custom-mixed syrups. And all the nuts Olympia uses are roasted in-house.

Olympia proudly notes on its website that its candies were "served at the Inaugural Ball of Presidents Ronald Reagan and George (H.W.) Bush." Kare says that came about with the assistance of an area congressman. "My brother drove a box truck full of candy to Washington, D.C.," he recalls.

Even for non-presidential patrons, Olympia ships its candies from coast to coast. The turtle is "far and away our best-seller," Kare says. Other popular items are the peanut clusters and chocolate-covered cherries. Seasonal treats include solid-chocolate hearts, peanut butter eggs and handmade candy canes. There are plenty of other non-chocolate options as well, such as gummies, jelly beans and licorice.

The Coca-Cola sign on the side of Olympia Candy Kitchen is a fixture dating to 1932. (Brian Tombaugh)

Both images: Kare Andersen is the fourth generation of his family to oversee the making of the chocolates, rum balls and other sandwiches and sweets at the Olympia Candy Kitchen. (Brian Tombaugh)

Trolley Café
1100 N. Chicago Avenue (the Old Bag Factory)
Goshen
(574) 534-3881

"Bagology": The word dominates the façade of Goshen's Old Bag Factory – a nod to the building's longtime history as home to the Chase Bag Factory. It was coined to reflect Chase's determination to raise bag production to the level of science. The days of bagology are long gone; Chase closed in 1982.

The 80,000-square-foot brick factory was built in 1896 as the Cosmo Buttermilk Soap Co. Chase took over in 1910 and, at its height, produced products ranging from waterproof burlap bags to the sheer paper wrappers for Hershey's Kisses candies. Today, the renovated building is home to an eclectic group of artists and merchants. Among the tastiest is the Trolley Café.

Both images: The restored Old Bag Factory of today retains much of the character of the building that started in 1896 as the Cosmo Buttermilk Soap Co. (Brian Tombaugh)

The café began as the Trolley Tea Room. Through a succession of owners, it evolved into a breakfast-and-lunch restaurant. Today the café is owned and run by Glenda Chupp and Brenda Johnson, who worked as waitresses before buying the business in 2004. "I never dreamed I'd own a restaurant," Glenda says.

Trolley Café employees make the breads, pies and muffins, as well as soups. Quiche is also a popular choice among diners. "We still have the original recipes," Glenda says.

Other food options throughout the Old Bag Factory include Bread & Chocolate, Sweet-Em's Cake Shop and The Chocolate Factory.

Right: The restored River Avenue Bridge across from the Old Bag Factory is a Pennsylvania through truss built in 1896. (Brian Tombaugh)

Below: A display at Goshen's Old Bag Factory shows an uncut roll of paper plumes for Hershey's Kisses candies. The plumes were made by the Chase Bag Factory from 1921 until 1982. (Brian Tombaugh)

Colombo's Italian Family Restaurant

2425 S. Main Street
Elkhart
(574) 293-6869

Colombo's smallish dining room can fill quickly with hungry diners enticed by the smells of fresh-baked bread and simmering homemade sauces. The choreography that then takes place among the staff can be mesmerizing to watch. From the kitchen to the table, employees move with effortless precision to deliver delicious pizzas, pastas and salads.

Co-owner Giuseppe (Joe) Siciliano arrived in Elkhart from Calabria, Italy, in 1969. After about a decade of work in Elkhart's recreational vehicle factories (and a trip back to his homeland, from which he returned with his bride), Joe and brother Domenico decided to go into business for themselves. They elected to name their business for the Italian word for "Columbus" after a random poll declared it the winner from among a number of possibilities.

Joe fondly recalls the day he was working in the hole that would become Colombo's basement banquet room ("We built this build-

Colombo's Italian Family Restaurant has been a fixture on Elkhart's Main Street for more than 30 years. (Brian Tombaugh)

ing with our hands ourselves," he says) when a man peered down to ask what was going on. When Joe said he was opening a restaurant, the man – as he receded back down the dirt pile – shook his head at the folly of starting a business in the depths of a recession.

But Colombo's proved popular as soon as it opened in 1981. "We got really busy from the beginning," Joe recalls. "The second weekend, we couldn't fill all the orders for pizzas."

The restaurant's website promises that Colombo's will "continue to bring our traditions to your table. Our special recipes ... have been passed down for generations."

Those generations remain in evidence around the dining room. "The whole family's worked here at one time or another," Joe says.

What has kept Colombo's food special for more than 30 years, he says, is attention to detail – fresh-cut vegetables and handmade dough. "If you've got something that works," he says, "don't try to reinvent it."

Below: Colombo's combo pizza features sausage, black olives, mushrooms, pepperoni, onions and green peppers on a cheese-smothered crust. (Brian Tombaugh)

(Brian Tombaugh)

New York Central Railroad Museum
721 S. Main Street
Elkhart
(574) 294-3001

The sound of a train whistle is common east of downtown Elkhart, where between 125 and 140 trains pass daily. Visitors to the New York Central Railroad Museum can whistle right back. A 1953 diesel-electric locomotive with a working whistle – the locomotive that made the final run of the 20th Century Limited – is a highlight for kids and kids at heart as they stroll through (and climb aboard) nearly a century and a half of railroad history.

But strolling isn't the only way to see the museum's treasures. Catch a ride on the miniature train that loops around a collection of rolling stock from different eras of railroading – from cranes to cabooses to boxcars. Among the museum's most treasured finds is a Mohawk steam locomotive that saw its first service out of Elkhart in 1940; it's billed as the largest surviving piece of the New York Central's modern steam technology. The locomotive, including its massive boiler with hundreds of large rivets, is being restored to its original gleaming brilliance.

An L3a 3001 Mohawk steam locomotive is a centerpiece of Elkhart's New York Central Railroad Museum. At a weight of 388,500 pounds and a boiler pressure of 250 psi, the locomotive is rated at 4,100 horsepower. (Brian Tombaugh)

Displays throughout the restored depot that houses the museum feature artifacts of railroad life from lanterns to dining car china. (Brian Tombaugh)

The New York Central's Robert R. Young Yard (now known as Norfolk Southern Railway's Elkhart Yard) is the largest railroad freight classification yard east of the Mississippi River. Amtrak's Capitol Limited and Lake Shore Limited also pass through daily. There's plenty of seating trackside if you want to pass the time watching the trains go by.

The city-owned museum opened in 1987, providing a link to when Elkhart saw its first train in 1851. Visitors from all 50 states and 18 foreign countries have taken the tour through the museum and its yards. Schoolchildren enjoy eating their lunch in the dining car that is part of the museum complex; the car also is available for luncheon rentals.

And there's plenty else to hold the attention of both the seasoned train lover and the young Thomas the Tank Engine fan. Artifacts on display range from track-layers' tools to conductors' lanterns to dishes from New York Central dining cars. An entire room is dedicated to a model train display, where several trains simultaneously weave their way through the intricately laid and breathtakingly decorated miniature landscape.

NEW YORK CENTRAL SYSTEM / NATIONAL NEW YORK CENTRAL RAILROAD MUSEUM WHEAT CAKES / PANCAKES

(Courtesy of Robin Hume)

2 egg yolks
2 cups milk
3 Tbsp. maple syrup
2 cups flour
½ tsp. salt
2 tsp. baking powder
5 Tbsp. butter

Beat egg yolks well. Continue to beat eggs as you slowly add milk, and then stir in your maple syrup. Sift together flour, salt and baking powder and add to egg mixture. Then stir in the melted butter. Stir until entire mixture is smooth. Let batter stand a few minutes before cooking. Cook pancakes on griddle and flip once only. ENJOY!!!!

The Lerner Theatre

410 S. Main Street
Elkhart
(574) 293-4469

From the "white-hot epicenter of the economic meltdown" arose this breathtaking jewel in the heart of Elkhart. "It's quite telling that the community hit hardest did this," says general manager David Smith of the restoration of The Lerner Theatre.

The city's economy (which was tied heavily to the recreational vehicle industry) took a huge hit in the Great Recession; at its worst, unemployment hovered near 20 percent. But citizens and civic leaders alike recognized the value of The Lerner. In 2008, the city approved an $18 million project to renovate the city-owned theater building and add a reception/ballroom space.

Residents were keen to hold onto a piece of history that commands the downtown streetscape with its Beaux Arts terra cotta façade accented by four columns. "This building was saved more for the past it represented than the future it held," David says. "It was the memories that saved it."

Those memories have been shaped since 1924, when Harry E. Lerner opened his 2,000-seat theater (the Thanksgiving Day opening feature was Buster Keaton's *The Navigator*). Elkhart's location as a rail hub between New York and Chicago also brought the biggest vaudeville acts of the Roaring '20s to The Lerner's door – Harry

Houdini and Al Jolson were among the big names to have made the stop. Through the decades, the building passed through several sets of hands (and several names, mainly the Elco) until the city took possession in 1990 to help stave off deterioration. (The Lerner had been designated a National Historical Landmark in 1980.)

Between 2009 and 2011, craftsmen painstakingly restored The Lerner to its pre-Depression grandeur. The original-print, red-and-gold wallpaper was re-created, plaster was remolded and patched, and the ceiling and mushroom chandeliers were repainted by hand. The 6,000-square-foot Crystal Ballroom rose on the site of a former jewelry store; it adjoins The Lerner and has a complementary décor. Also receiving a renovation was The Lerner's 1,124-pipe Kimball organ, one of only a few that remain at the site of its original installation.

"A Week of Celebration" in June 2011 welcomed the public back to its theater with a series of free performances, from *Fiddler on the Roof* to gospel night.

"We're creating the memories that can save the place 80 years from now," David says. "It's a continuum of care."

The dancing Lerner Lady – the theater's symbol – can be seen on the lobby floor as well as on light fixtures outside the building and on aisle seats in the auditorium. (Brian Tombaugh)

Since its reopening in 2011 following a complete restoration, the stage at The Lerner Theatre has hosted both national acts and local productions. (Brian Tombaugh)

The Security Building served as a series of banks; the former vault has been turned into a 10-seat private dining room. (Brian Tombaugh)

The Vine
214 S. Main Street
Elkhart
(574) 970-5006

The Security Building stands out along the streetscape of the Lincoln Highway as the road makes its way through downtown Elkhart. Built in 1892, the red sandstone and brick Chateauesque, copper-roofed building has been home to a number of banks through the years. Other uses have included a funeral parlor, a World War II-era rationing office and the River of Life Christian Church. These days, it's home to the second of two restaurants known as The Vine.

The Elkhart location, opened in March 2007, is the second for Jamie DeVinney and executive chef Doug Schultz. A downtown South Bend restaurant opened in November 1998. The goal, Doug says, is simply "good-quality food for a reasonable price."

"We don't have a deep fryer," he adds. "You're going to get good, quality stuff."

A particular feature of the restaurant is a private dining room fashioned out of the former bank vault; that vault sits atop a 10-foot-thick slab of concrete and is surrounded by brick that is five layers thick, researchers have found. The room seats up to 10 people in a cozy space decorated with a vineyard mural and wine bottles arranged on racks. The Vine also accommodates private parties and wine-tasting dinners.

Left: For more than a century, the façade of the building that is now home to The Vine restaurant has stood watch over downtown Elkhart. (Brian Tombaugh)

moving a drop ceiling revealed a tin ceiling for which replacement tiles were locally made. The grocery's old meat locker now functions as the Old Style's walk-in cooler.

Janice's memories are stored in a stuffed, green scrapbook that she pulls from behind the counter. In addition to old menus and newspaper clippings, her scrapbook contains photos of some of her regulars. These days, she's serving some second-generation customers, as well.

Left: Both the artwork (featuring Hoosier favorite son David Letterman front and center) and the sandwich names (Farmer in the Deli, anyone?) hint at the whimsy of the Old Style Deli. (Brian Tombaugh)

Below: The Old Style Deli, now in its third location, has been serving downtown Elkhart for more than 30 years. (Brian Tombaugh)

Old Style Deli
200 S. Main Street
Elkhart
(574) 295-2133

"No sniveling" reads the sign over the counter at Janice Hayden's Old Style Deli. It's part of an atmosphere that invites you to sit down and enjoy yourself. Grab a magazine off the rack just inside the front door as you wait for your David Letterman (roast beef), Popeye pocket (chicken and spinach) or eggsclusive (just what it sounds like) club sandwich.

Freshly made soups are another Old Style Deli specialty, where everything is made from scratch. "I love making soup," Janice says. "We get a lot of people commenting on how good the soup is."

Janice has run the Old Style at three different locations since taking ownership in 1983. Her current corner location was once home to a grocery store; she refurbished it with the help of her husband. Re-

A former Studebaker dealership in downtown Mishawaka has been repurposed, but the company's influence on the area remains evident. (Brian Tombaugh)

The Studebaker name — synonymous with the automobile — can first be found in South Bend in 1852, when the H&C Studebaker blacksmith shop opened. The company's first automobiles (in 1902) were electric, a gas-powered version was introduced two years later. Production in South Bend continued through 1963; Studebaker was out of business by 1966. A museum in the city commemorates Studebaker's contributions to South Bend, northern Indiana and the nation.

St. Joseph
COUNTY

OUT OF THE PAST

Lincoln Highway Inn
2754 Lincoln Way East
Mishawaka

Mishawaka's Lincoln Highway Inn and Restaurant on Lincolnway East was famous for its salad dressing.

(Courtesy Russell Rein)

LINCOLN HIGHWAY INN SALAD DRESSING

Combine:

1 can tomato soup
½ cup vinegar
½ cup oil
¾ cup sugar
1 Tbsp. dry mustard
1 Tbsp. Worcestershire sauce
1 grated onion
1 Tbsp. paprika
1 Tbsp. garlic salt
1 Tbsp. pepper

Featured Landmark

Mishawaka High School
1202 Lincoln Way East
Mishawaka
(574) 254-7300

Mishawaka High School graduate Sharon Versyp was Indiana's 1984 Miss Basketball. She is now the women's basketball coach at Purdue University. Graduate Adam Driver found fame in 2015 as Kylo Ren in *Star Wars: The Force Awaken*s.

On the north side of the highway, east of downtown Mishawaka, sits the imposing and inspiring Mishawaka High School building with its signature clock tower. The 1924 building, along with its additions and stadium, cover a four-square-block area of 16⅓ acres. The school is home to roughly 1,700 students in grades 9 through 12; its athletic teams are known as the Cavemen.

"The grounds were carefully planned by landscape gardeners before the building was built," reports a history of the building on the high school's website. Renovations in 1959 and 1963 added additional gym space and an academic wing, respectively. The two-floor gym seats nearly 4,000. A series of indoor and outdoor modernizations were completed between 1976 and 1980.

Additional classroom and music room space was added in 1984, and a science/technology wing (complete with television studio) was finished in 1999.

The 319,949-square-foot Mishawaka High School, completed in 1924, was built at a cost of $800,000. (Brian Tombaugh)

Summertime outdoor seating alongside the sign that gave the restaurant its name is a popular attraction at Doc Pierce's. (Brian Tombaugh)

Doc Pierce's

120 N. Main Street
Mishawaka
(574) 255-7737

A sense of fun permeates this place, starting with the name. Dr. Ray Vaughn Pierce practiced in Pennsylvania and New York in the post-Civil War years and was known for creating and selling patent medicines. The "golden medical discovery" advertised on the side of the building that now carries his name was guaranteed to "cure weak women." (The concoction was said to contain honey, tincture of digitalis and the extract of acrid poisonous lettuce; it was 64 percent alcohol.)

Doc Pierce and his medicines were long forgotten until a 1976 fire burned down the furniture store next door shortly after the building had been bought for conversion into a restaurant, revealing a ghosted sign.

The antique stained glass that dominates the décor was the find of Coy Jankowski, an artist who was one of the restaurant's three original co-owners. Other decorative touches include Tiffany-style lights over each table (no two are alike), the massive gearworks of an old elevator, a fireplace and a mounted carousel horse. Exposed brick and dark tongue-and-groove plank paneling complete the steakhouse feel.

"'The place for steaks' is what we've called ourselves for years," says manager T.J. Laughlin, who quickly adds, "our onion rings kinda put us on the map."

Lincolnway Café

2524 Lincolnway West
Mishawaka
(574) 256-7024

At the Lincolnway Café, the customers are as much of the experience as the large collection of enamelware or the "Beware of Attack Waitress" sign on the wood-plank walls. "It's one of those places where people still talk to each other," says owner Stacey Glassburn-Wilson. "They put their iPhones down."

"There aren't too many places like (this) anymore," she adds, "and they're rapidly falling away."

Stacey estimates that about 75 percent of her diners are once-a-week regulars; half of them are in three or more days out of the six that the café is open (it's closed on Mondays). "We have customers call if they know they're not going to be in," she says. "They know we care." (She pauses at one point in the conversation to ask about the health of a pregnant customer.)

The atmosphere is casual – if not beyond. "We kinda fly by the seat of our pants here," Stacey says.

Your menu hangs on a wall hook next to your table. The daily specials are posted on a whiteboard; soups of the day are listed on a chalkboard. Need a coffee refill? Help yourself. Find a unique hot sauce while on vacation? Be sure to bring some back to share.

MINESTRONE SOUP

(courtesy of Stacey Glassburn-Wilson / Lincolnway Café)

This is a restaurant favorite – especially in the summer, when all the veggies in my home garden become available. Fresh is always best and adds something to the soup's flavor, but feel free to swap out frozen or canned in the same proportions. This is one of those magic soups that you can change, add, leave out and switch up in all sorts of ways to suit your family's tastes. Enjoy!

Base broth:

4 cups tomato juice
5 cups chicken stock or vegetable stock
2 Tbsp. fresh oregano
4 Tbsp. fresh basil
1 tsp. fresh thyme
1 tsp. fresh parsley
2 bay leaves
½ tsp. black pepper

Mix together in a stock pot and bring to simmer slowly.

Sauté together:

1 cup chopped celery
½ cup carrots, diced (heirloom carrots in a variety of colors add a pretty touch)
1 cup onion, chopped (I mix red, green and white onions from the garden)
1 cup zucchini, cubed or, if young, sliced ¼ inch
1 cup yellow squash, cubed
1 cup diced tomatoes (yellow, red, heirloom, cherry, roma and the more the merrier. Juice and seeds, too!)
1 Tbsp. diced garlic or crushed cloves

Just enough olive oil or bacon drippings to lightly sauté until onions are translucent
Add to simmering broth mixture immediately.

Final touches:

1 cup finely ground cooked, drained Italian sausage (can be left out for a great vegetarian option)
2 cups coarsely chopped spinach or Swiss chard
4 Tbsp. grated Parmesan or Romano cheese
3 cups cooked pasta, al dente (I use ditalini, but any shape will do)
1 large can cannellini beans (white kidney beans or navy will do, as well), rinsed and drained

Simmer altogether until veggies are tender. Garnish with fresh, diced basil and a shake of Parmesan cheese.

"It's kinda like my home away from home," Stacey Glassburn-Wilson says of her Lincolnway Café. (Brian Tombaugh)

The specials include "normally something that's not on the menu," Stacey says, and pancakes are likely to be one of the features. "I have a thing about recipes for pancakes," she says. Some of her special ingredients have included Oreos, Reese's Pieces and Snickers. Red velvet, carrot cake and banana nut pancakes have been tasty options, as well. Biscuits and gravy are another specialty.

The restaurant sits where a two-story home once did. The building was a dairy office and a Taco John's restaurant before it became the Lincolnway Café in 1990. The café has been Stacey's for several years; she's been waitressing since age 14.

The café doesn't close too often, including on many holidays. "I want to make sure people have a place to go," Stacey says. "You might as well feel at home."

A chalkboard and a white board keep Stacey Glassburn-Wilson's customers apprised of the daily specials at Lincolnway Café. (Brian Tombaugh)

Bonnie Doon

2704 Lincoln Way West
Mishawaka
(574) 255-9841

The Bonnie Doon chain had as many as nine drive-ins throughout St. Joseph and Elkhart counties. But the truth is that there never was a Bonnie Doon. The company was formed in 1938 by brothers Herman and Andrew Muldoon; Bonnie Doon was selected as the winner in a naming contest from nearly 400 entries.

The Lincoln Way location is the lone remaining drive-in. In the mid-1940s, Bonnie Doon became the first restaurant in the area to have drive-ins and carhops. The stores once sold sundaes for a dime, and quart "bricks" of ice cream cost 30 cents.

Among the treats still available in-store is Bonnie Doon's Banana Boat. It consists of sliced bananas topped by two or three scoops of your choice of ice cream flavors. That is covered with both strawberry and pineapple toppings, as well as nuts, whipped cream and a cherry.

In 1990, the company was acquired by Sam Dugan. Four years later, Sam moved ice cream production to a converted Indiana Toll Road building in Elkhart. (Bonnie Doon ice cream also is available at area grocery stores.)

Rapport with customers remains as strong as when ice cream fans gave Bonnie Doon its name. In 1994, faced with rising production costs, Sam needed either to raise the price or reduce the carton size. So he put the question to the public. The *South Bend Tribune* reported in 2011: "Customers spoke up, and the carton size was reduced and the price stayed the same."

Bonnie Doon's traditional banana split features your choice of two flavors of ice cream along with whipped cream, nuts and a maraschino cherry. (Brian Tombaugh)

A hand-lettered sign from a now-closed location listed the flavors available to Bonnie Doon's drive-through customers. (Brian Tombaugh)

A post-1928 view of the South Bend Farmer's Market shows essentially the same configuration that is in use today. (Courtesy South Bend Farmer's Market)

South Bend Farmer's Market

1105 Northside Blvd.
South Bend
(574) 282-1259

South Bend Farmer's Market sits just across the Sample Street bridge to the northeast of Lincoln Way – which is somewhat appropriate, since the farmer's market started out on a bridge.

In July 1911, the market opened for business on the city's Colfax Street bridge. The year-round market operated from dawn to 10 a.m. on Tuesday, Thursday and Saturday, drawing sellers from a 40-mile radius. (There are now also Friday hours in late May through September. The market is open from 7 a.m. to 2 p.m., and to 3 p.m. on Saturday.)

By 1923, the market had outgrown its bridge. "There were often more than 100 sellers and thousands of buyers on a single day," according to the market's website. After incorporating in 1924 and five years at another location, the market settled into its Northside Boulevard home in 1928. Today's 96-stall building has been in place since 1972, after a 1971 fire destroyed part of the earlier market. A three-counter restaurant is situated in the cross portion of the H-shaped structure.

The market bills itself as "one of the largest and most diverse indoor markets in the Midwest."

"Over the years, the Farmer's Market has been known as the best spot to purchase farm-grown vegetables, a unique variety of cheeses, eggs and meats, fresh fish and lamb, artisan baked goods, maple syrup, the highest quality fruits, homemade candies, floral bouquets, handcrafted jewelry and numerous other items," the website boasts.

ROSA MARINA SOUP

(courtesy of Hiatt's Poultry, LLC / South Bend Farmer's Market)

5-6 green onions
2 large celery stalks
1 large carrot (¾ cup)
3 cups chicken broth
½ cup orzo pasta
salt

pepper
garlic powder
parsley
basil
24 oz. V8 juice

Chop green onions, celery stalks and carrot; place in broth and add orzo. Add salt, pepper, garlic powder, parsley and basil. Cook slowly for a half-hour. Add V8 juice; heat and serve.

OUT OF THE PAST

A&W Root Beer barrel

705 Lincolnway West
South Bend

Long gone from near the southern end of the Sample Street bridge is one of A&W's famed barrel-shaped root beer stands. By the 1960s, the barrel had been razed, according to Jan Shupert-Arick's *The Lincoln Highway across Indiana*; the site was converted to a drive-in restaurant with carhops as well as indoor seating.

Children line up to hand over their nickel for a mug of "ice cold A&W Root Beer." (Courtesy The History Museum)

Café Navarre

101 N. Michigan Street
South Bend
(574) 968-8101

At the intersection of the Lincoln and Dixie highways, you'll find Café Navarre, which itself is an intersection of classic architecture and contemporary upscale dining.

"A lot of history has happened on this corner," says Elaine Thibault, Café Navarre's one-time hospitality and events coordinator. During John Dillinger's last confirmed bank holdup in June 1934, a security guard was slain outside the building at the intersection of Michigan and Washington streets.

The Renaissance-style Café Navarre building still bears the name of American Trust, the bank that opened at the corner in 1904. (It had changed hands by the time of the Dillinger job.) The Indiana limestone building on the site today replaced the original bank building in 1924. The safe deposit box in the basement – billed as the largest in Indiana in its day – weighed 19 tons.

Underneath the 24-foot ceiling once stood 19 marble and bronze teller cages; they have been replaced by dining tables. A mezzanine that overhangs the space is the only significant alteration made during the 2011 renovation of the National Register of Historic Places building by owner and noted South Bend/Elkhart restaurateur and philanthropist Kurt Janowsky. In addition to seating, this upper level affords access to three private dining areas: the Clock Room, the Teller's Cage and the boardroom-style John Malpass Room.

Café Navarre opened in January 2012. The restaurant is named in honor of Pierre Navarre, one of South Bend's first European settlers. Kurt chose the winning name from among hundreds of submissions to a *South Bend Tribune* newspaper contest.

Café Navarre's French Onion Gratinee soup – with its top layer of aged Gruyere – is served with a toasted baguette. (Brian Tombaugh)

Both images: *The long, some-what shallow space that once functioned as the bank lobby has been converted into a two-level, upscale dining room. (Brian Tombaugh)*

The menu includes French, Spanish and Italian influences. "We're very well-known for our seafood," adds general manager John Dawson. "We have fresh fish flown in every day."

Patrons run the gamut from congressional reps to performers from the nearby Morris Center for the Performing Arts to travelers drawn by the café's rave online reviews. In the first two years after Café Navarre opened, "downtown has just embraced us," Elaine says. Toward that end, the restaurant instituted a monthly charity giveback. Agencies that have benefitted include the Salvation Army, the Center for the Homeless and the Christmas Commandos.

"We have adventures happening all the time," she says.

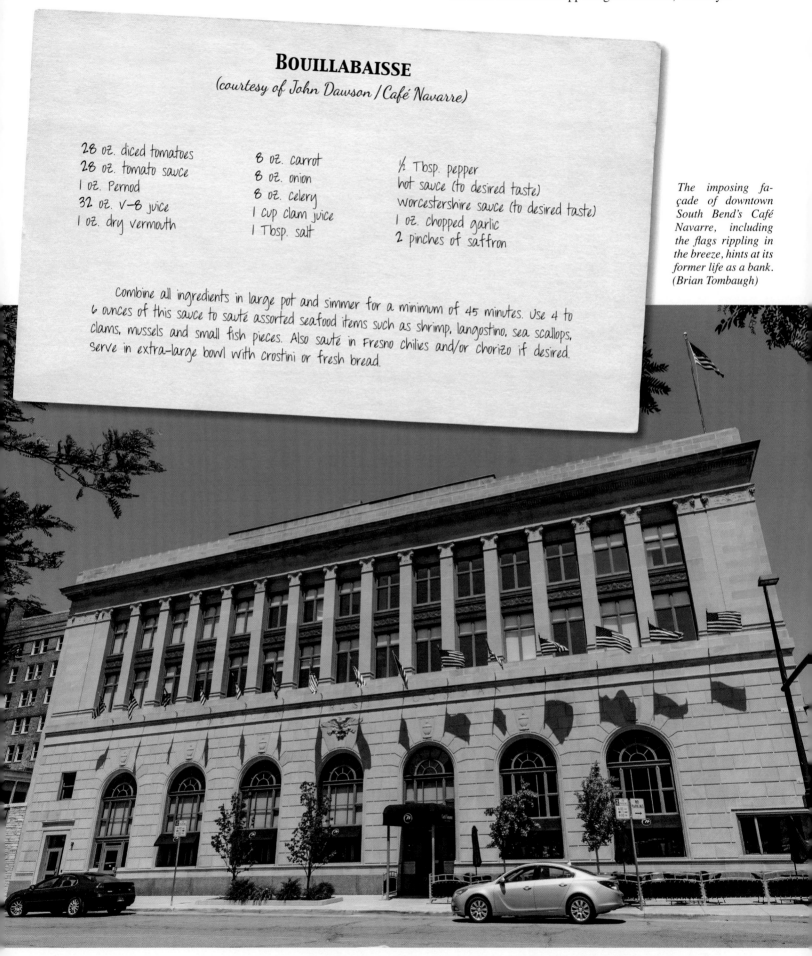

BOUILLABAISSE

(courtesy of John Dawson / Café Navarre)

28 oz. diced tomatoes
28 oz. tomato sauce
1 oz. Pernod
32 oz. V-8 juice
1 oz. dry vermouth

8 oz. carrot
8 oz. onion
8 oz. celery
1 cup clam juice
1 Tbsp. salt

½ Tbsp. pepper
hot sauce (to desired taste)
worcestershire sauce (to desired taste)
1 oz. chopped garlic
2 pinches of saffron

Combine all ingredients in large pot and simmer for a minimum of 45 minutes. Use 4 to 6 ounces of this sauce to sauté assorted seafood items such as shrimp, langostino, sea scallops, clams, mussels and small fish pieces. Also sauté in Fresno chilies and/or chorizo if desired. Serve in extra-large bowl with crostini or fresh bread.

The imposing façade of downtown South Bend's Café Navarre, including the flags rippling in the breeze, hints at its former life as a bank. (Brian Tombaugh)

The Moderne
110 N. Michigan Street
South Bend

Edward N. Kalamaros opened The Moderne in 1927; the restaurant that featured a Czechoslovakian stained-glass window over its front entrance was a downtown South Bend fixture for 40 years.

South Bend's Center for History describes The Moderne thusly: "Customers were tempted by an array of candies, pastries and ice cream concoctions all made on the premises and displayed in the cases and soda fountain at the front of the store, or if they chose, they could be seated in the back half of the restaurant at tables and booths for lunch."

An intricately detailed stained-glass window greeted visitors to downtown South Bend's Moderne for four decades. The lavishly decorated hearts in the windows offer a clue as to the timing of this photo. (Courtesy The History Museum)

Edward arrived in Moline, Illinois, from Greece at age 16. He made his way to Michigan City, where he sold ice and sodas in a park. He also learned to make candy.

The multistory Moderne had floors dedicated to candy-making and baking. "The store also served food and ice cream. The light salads and lunches were popular with downtown workers," according to a 2013 Center for History exhibit. "The store was a family affair," it adds, "with (Edward's) children working in the shop and at the counters."

Georgiana Bennett had her own memories of The Moderne. In 1999, she recalled for the *South Bend Tribune*: "South Bend was a real town then. People dressed up to come downtown. Ladies wore hats and gloves and met for lunch at The Moderne, a wonderful candy and soda shop with black and white octagon tile floors and glass case after glass case of fancy chocolates. It had a real soda fountain, where you could get cherry phosphates, black cows, victory splits and chocolate malts. It had booths in the back and a mezzanine, too."

OUT OF THE PAST

The Philadelphia
116 N. Michigan Street
South Bend

Philadelphia, Pennsylvania, is where the Poledor brothers learned the art of candy-making after they emigrated from their native Greece. So in 1901, when Eustice, Andrew and Pendel decided to open their own shop in South Bend, Indiana, the choice of names was obvious.

The Poledors joined in as the confectionary business boomed in South Bend. The *South Bend Tribune* noted that by 1912, the city was home to 59 candy businesses; two generations earlier, there had been but one.

In its day, The Philadelphia made its own ice cream in the basement, served both lunch and dinner on the first floor, made pastries on the second floor and made candies on the third floor (in a total of more than 20,000 square feet of space). A soda fountain – added in 1930 – was a big draw for students out on dates from Notre Dame or Saint Mary's College.

The Philadelphia grew steadily through the years, once producing as much as 500 pounds of candy and 200 gallons of ice cream a day. The Poledors expanded three times in their first decade and remodeled in 1940 and 1955. The restaurant's mirrored walls and barrel-vault ceiling gave the space the impression of being even larger than it was.

"It looked a lot like a Pullman railroad car," Ted Poledor told the *South Bend Tribune* in 2001. Ted, a son of Pendel, was part of the second generation to run The Philadelphia; he rose from a soda fountain operator.

The 1963 closure of South Bend's Studebaker plant, which left more than 7,000 people jobless, signaled a downturn for the city. In 1971, the block on which The Philadelphia sat was acquired through eminent domain. The building was torn down two years later as part of a downtown revitalization effort that never materialized. The excavation was known locally as "the hole" until a Marriott opened on the site in 1981. A bank also now occupies the site.

Ted reopened The Philadelphia at a new location in 1986 and ran it until 2002. New owners kept the store open until 2009.

A 2013 Center for History exhibit on area candy-makers included the Philadelphia's ribbon candy-making machine and cookbooks featuring recipes in both English and Greek.

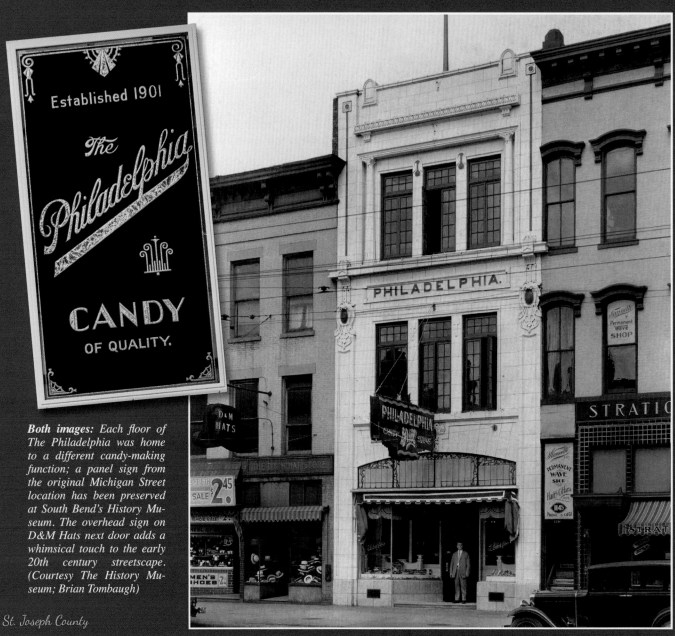

Both images: Each floor of The Philadelphia was home to a different candy-making function; a panel sign from the original Michigan Street location has been preserved at South Bend's History Museum. The overhead sign on D&M Hats next door adds a whimsical touch to the early 20th century streetscape. (Courtesy The History Museum; Brian Tombaugh)

Established 1901

The Philadelphia

CANDY
OF QUALITY.

PHILADELPHIA.

Tippecanoe Place
620 W. Washington Street
South Bend
(574) 234-9077

At the start of the 20th century, Clement Studebaker's home was South Bend's social hub. "He loved to throw a good party," says Sherri Huffer. "He loved to entertain." Tippecanoe Place, where Sherri is general manager, carries on the tradition; for more than 30 years, it's been hosting dinner for up to 500 guests. As Sherri is quick to point out, though, "We're an attraction as well as a restaurant. People come in and see the surroundings and just marvel."

The Studebaker family settled into its 26,000-square-foot home in 1889, following three years of construction. The house cost $250,000 (plus another $100,000 for furnishings). The Studebakers had lived at Tippecanoe Place less than a year when fire struck the top floor. That level contained an art gallery, but the space was converted to a ballroom after the fire claimed most of the artwork.

The home's centerpiece is its extra-wide grand staircase, which guests descended to make their entrance. German craftsmen spent a year on the details of the hand-carved oak masterpiece. The mansion's iron-cage elevator still serves the restaurant today. Sherri boasts that it's the third oldest in the nation, behind only those in the White House and the home of Otis Elevator founder Elisha Otis.

Both images: The 1889 fieldstone Clement Studebaker mansion, with its intricately carved detailing, was designated a National Historic Landmark in 1978. (Brian Tombaugh)

Other notable features include an 86-by-20-foot formal dining room that seats up to 100 people (its walls and ceiling decorated in Moroccan leather) and a single-lane bowling alley in a subbasement.

"This family was royalty back then," Sherri says.

Clement Studebaker and his brother Henry found success as wagon builders and blacksmiths – they were major suppliers of the Union Army during the Civil War. The Studebaker company later became one of the few to make the successful transition from the wagon to the automobile.

In an earlier age, guests of the Studebaker family at Tippecanoe Place made their entry by descending the grand staircase that now dominates the restaurant's lobby. (Brian Tombaugh)

But the Great Depression beset the Studebakers as it did so many other American families. Their granite, fieldstone home was shuttered when Clement's son George, to whom the mansion had passed, declared bankruptcy in 1933. Its furnishings were sold off to satisfy debtors, but the house remained unsold. It went through incarnations as a Red Cross headquarters, a home for "crippled children" and a museum until it was acquired by the Ralston Purina Corporation in 1979 (a year after the house had been declared a national historic landmark) to be converted into a restaurant. Since 2008, Tippecanoe Place has been privately owned by the Matteoni family.

"It's old," Sherri says of the home. "It needs a lot of love. The new owners have put a lot of love in."

The restaurant, which specializes in prime rib, draws a significant number of Lincoln Highway travelers ("We get people all the time driving that original route," Sherri says), as well as Studebaker enthusiasts. "That's one of the cool things about this job," she adds. "You meet people from all over the world."

Both images: *A grilled French-cut pork chop with roasted vegetables and a wedge salad as a starter make for an enjoyable Tippecanoe Place meal. (Brian Tombaugh)*

FRANGELICO MOUSSE
(courtesy of Tippecanoe Place)

1 lb. cream cheese
1 cup sugar
½ cup Frangelico Liqueur
2 cups whipped cream (aerosols can be used or whip fresh)

Cut cream cheese into 1-ounce cubes. Let soften at room temperature for 20 minutes. Start with half in a mixing bowl and blend on medium. Add sugar and the rest of the cream cheese one cube at a time. Stop and scrape sides down, then whip on high for 3 minutes. Add liqueur (or hazelnut oil if you do not want alcohol). Fold together with whipped cream, pipe into serving dish and let set up under refrigeration.

Below: The Gilded Age elegance of Tippecanoe Place, including its rich woods, mirrored fireplaces and ornate chandeliers, has been faithfully restored and preserved. (Brian Tombaugh)

The Inn at the Old Republic

304 E. Michigan Street
New Carlisle
(574) 654-8199

The Old Republic stands guard over the Lincoln Highway's eastern entrance into New Carlisle. Through its 150-year history, it has survived conversion into apartments, a stint as a used-car lot and a date with the wrecking ball. Today, it's a restored treasure housing a museum as well as a bed and breakfast.

The Italianate brick home topped by an anachronistic onion dome commands a hilltop view. On that site in 1860, local farmer Jeremiah Service – a banker and dry goods store owner in later years – chose to build his family home. The building remained a residence until the late 1960s, when an auto dealer decided to open his lot on the lawn. The next owner let the property deteriorate for more than 30 years.

In 1989, the house garnered screen time in the movie *Prancer*. Its ramshackle appearance was deemed perfect for the home of Cloris Leachman's Mrs. McFarland.

By 1998, town officials were ready to order demolition. Historic New Carlisle was given a final opportunity to save the Old Republic and, with financial assistance from Historic Landmarks of Indiana, took possession of the building.

"We felt that the house belonged to the community," says Dana Groves, Historic New Carlisle's executive director.

A more than $1 million renovation, begun in 2001, restored the home to its present-day glory. No original furnishings remain; all that is in use at the Old Republic today has been donated. "It was kind of just a blank canvas," Dana recalls. "There was nothing decorative left in the house for us."

Luncheons, weddings and teas are common on the first floor; on the second floor are four bedrooms, named after the four Service children who lived to adulthood. Personal items donated by Jeremiah's great-great-great-grandsons are on display, while Service family photos adorn the hallway connecting the four bedrooms upstairs.

Still in the works are plans to restore an icehouse and a smokehouse on the grounds. At Historic New Carlisle's museum, in the rear of the building, you can view town artifacts and buy cookbooks full of recipes featured at The Inn.

CHICKEN TEA SANDWICHES
(courtesy of Nancy Taplin / Teatime on the Hill cookbook)

2 cups cubed cooked chicken
¾ cup dried cranberries
¼ cup chopped pecans
1 medium unpeeled red apple, chopped
½ cup thinly sliced celery
2 Tbsp. sliced green onion
¾ cup mayonnaise or salad dressing
2 tsp. lime juice

In a bowl, combine everything except mayonnaise and lime juice. In a separate bowl, combine mayo and juice and add to chicken mixture; stir to coat. Cover bread of choice and serve open-faced.

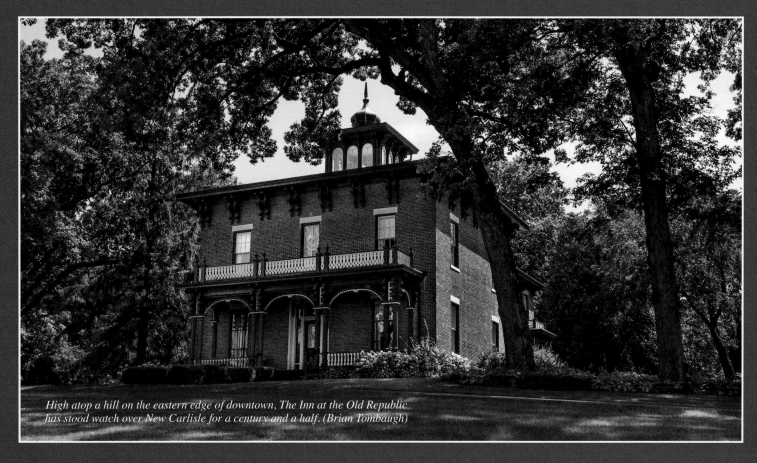

High atop a hill on the eastern edge of downtown, The Inn at the Old Republic has stood watch over New Carlisle for a century and a half. (Brian Tombaugh)

Both images: *Meghan Czarnecki tends to the counter at Carlisle Coffee & Sweets, where baked treats, truffles and Italian sodas all are available. (Brian Tombaugh)*

Caramel Truffles

Chocolate Truffles

Coconut Truffles

Raspberry Truffles

Amaretto Truffles

Carlisle Coffee & Sweets

203 E. Michigan Street
New Carlisle
(574) 307-4989

Following dinner at Moser's Austrian Cafe (see following entry), a stroll through the brick archway into the shop next door offers additional temptation for your sweet tooth.

Carlisle Coffee & Sweets features homemade Palazzolo's gelato and Veni's chocolates (imported from Niles, Michigan). The baked goods – from muffins to brownies to cheesecake to cannolis – are from the backroom kitchen of Margaret Czarnecki.

Margaret's husband, Derrick, teamed with John Antonucci in the restoration of the adjacent buildings. Derrick is an electrician by trade, a skill that proved handy as the building was gutted. "We took it down to the rafters," Derrick recalls. "We basically started from scratch."

The building "has had some uses over the years," he says. It had been an appliance store, auto parts store and chiropractor's office. The site was originally New Carlisle's post office; at one time, the town postmaster was Schuyler Colfax, first vice president under Ulysses S. Grant and a former Speaker of the House.

The 2010-11 renovation was closely watched in the town of 1,850. "People just saw us hauling stuff in and hauling stuff out," Derrick says.

"They were just dying to know (what was going on)," adds Margaret. "It was really neat to watch the transition," she says. "So many people knew this building."

A steady clientele has developed since Carlisle Coffee & Sweets' opening.

With daughter Meghan home from college in San Diego, the counter is well-tended. (People come in and ask, "Are you hiring, or do you have to be family?" Margaret says.) And don't tell the health department, but on some Saturday mornings, golden Labrador Maddie might be there carrying her leash in her mouth, dropping it only long enough to accept the occasional gummi worm.

Moser's Austrian Cafe

201 E. Michigan Street
New Carlisle
(574) 654-0086

If you're in the mood for schnitzel, then Moser's Austrian Cafe is where you want to be. Twelve different varieties await you. "It's all authentic stuff," says owner Werner Moser. "From the old country."

That would be Bad Hofgastein, Austria. Werner tries to make it back to his Austrian Alps hometown at least once a year. Frequently, he leads a tour group to Europe and uses the town as a base for a visit to Vienna or Venice.

Werner was a ski instructor in Austria before his first visit to the United States in 1979 (he moved to America permanently in 1982). And he was familiar with the service industry; his family runs a bed and breakfast in Bad Hofgastein.

Moser's servers sport authentic Alpine dresses. Dressed in lederhosen (ignore the flip-flops), Werner comes out from the kitchen to greet his guests.

German and Austrian dishes are his specialty, but American food is available at Moser's, as well. And as Werner explains, there is a difference between German and Austrian cuisine: German is more bland. Austrian food reflects the diversity of the Austro-Hungarian Empire; proximity to Italy also helped spice up Austrian dishes.

Both images above: *A typical Moser's dinner is likely to include all the German favorites: sausage, sauerkraut, potatoes and spaetzle, all topped off with a slice of strudel. (Brian Tombaugh)*

That adventurousness is reflected in Moser's soups. Among Werner's creations are radish, garlic, spicy peanut butter and Reuben. Pastries are the work of a culinary school-trained chef (with an assist from Frau Moser, who herself helps out in the kitchen when she's visiting).

And of course, there's beer; it's all imported. "People come in and want Miller Lite or Bud Light, and I tell them, 'All we have is good beer,'" Werner says.

The building that houses Moser's has its own story to tell. John Antonucci and a pair of partners spent 11 months on restoration efforts. That effort won them the 2011 Rehabilitation Award from Historic New Carlisle.

A polished wooden floor offsets the exposed brick walls (four bricks thick). Nearly floor-to-ceiling windows across the front invite patrons to watch the traffic pass as they dine. A wooden staircase with a wrought-iron railing leads to a second floor with additional dining space, as well as a huge wooden bar.

Ripping the façade off the former antique store – which had earlier incarnations as a pharmacy, firehouse, post office and dry goods store – revealed a long-hidden decorative iron post. It also revealed a huge structural issue. "We found there was no foundation holding up the second floor," John, a Notre Dame-educated architect, recalls.

"It's a 125-year-old building that's brand new," John says.

Though Moser's Austrian Cafe and Carlisle Coffee & Sweets are adjoined both outside and inside, they offer vastly different temptations for the taste buds. (Brian Tombaugh)

Miller's Home Cafe has offered home-cooked meals for more than 50 years. (Brian Tombaugh)

Miller's Home Cafe
110 E. Michigan Street
New Carlisle
(574) 654-3431

"Smorgasbord" is the operative word at Miller's Home Cafe, where George Miller carries on the tradition begun by his parents in 1959.

Two generous buffet lines, kept brimming by George and members of his family, await diners as they are seated. Among the mainstays for both the smorgasbord and the lunch buffet are homemade noodles (the recipe "has been in the family a long time," George says), mashed potatoes, dressing, fried chicken and Polish sausage. Among the specialty items, depending on the day, are barbecued ribs and sautéed chicken livers. "Most everything is homemade," George says, including all the salads – macaroni, potato and pickled beets, among others.

George's parents, William and Vula Miller, moved to New Carlisle in 1949. Ten years later, William (also known as Big Bill) bought and opened the café in an 1890s-vintage building as a 60-seat diner where the smorgasbord was available only on Sunday. In 1968, William bought the hardware store directly to the east and expanded. A final addition to the café – bringing the capacity to 220 – was completed in 1978. All these years later, it's still referred to as "the new room," George jokes.

In 1980, George and his brother, William Jr., took over daily operations, though as their website's history tells it, "you could still find Big Bill in the kitchen more often than not preparing some of the family recipes." William Jr. retired in 2008.

Employees not named Miller have remained loyal, too – two of the cooks have been there for more than 30 years and one of the waitresses for 23 years. Customers are just as loyal. Regulars make the trip from Chicago, South Bend/Mishawaka, Valparaiso, Chesterton and LaPorte. Others who have visited include legendary Ohio State football coach Woody Hayes and film critic Roger Ebert.

Miller's also supplies food for parties and other gatherings. An order of eight gallons of noodles and 150 pieces of fried chicken for a graduation party is not uncommon.

(Brian Tombaugh)

Concrete markers, such as one on display at the LaPorte County Historical Society Museum, were placed by the Boy Scouts along the highway route in 1928. Designed by landscape architect Jens Jensen, the reinforced markers featured the Lincoln Highway logo, a cast bronze medallion and directional arrows. According to historian Jan Shupert-Arick, the Boy Scouts placed more than 2,400 such markers along the coast-to-coast route.

LaPorte

COUNTY

Hudson Lake
New Carlisle

At the height of the Roaring '20s, the dance bands of Benny Goodman and Guy Lombardo echoed on the shores of Hudson Lake. Many a Lincoln Highway traveler was likely lured into a side trip to hear the jazz sounds of Bix Beiderbecke and Jean Goldkette.

The dance hall first called The Casino opened in 1914. W.J. Smith added the dance spot as a companion to the 30-room hotel he had opened at Hudson Lake in the 1890s. The hotel came down in 1960, and The Casino went through incarnations as a roller skating rink, auction site and boathouse before being bought and renovated by Don and Barb Davis in 2001.

In its day, the Casino drew patrons from as far as Chicago, who arrived on the South Shore interurban line. The ballroom commands a view of Hudson Lake's 432 acres from a bank of windows at the end opposite the stage.

A 10,000-square-foot wooden dance floor has room for at least 600 couples. (Brian Tombaugh)

Junction City Restaurant

5636 E. U.S. 20
Rolling Prairie
(574) 778-2813

Hiram Mitchell is a man on the move. If he's not hauling freight for Landstar Trucking, you're just as likely to find him perched on a road grader, smoothing out the gravel at the parking lot of his Rolling Prairie truck stop/restaurant.

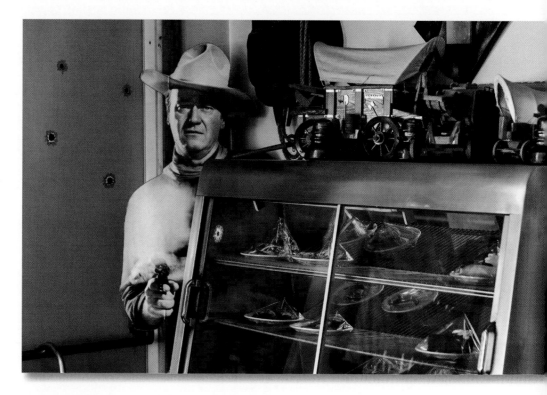

Having dodged the "bullets" embedded in the wall behind him, "John Wayne" stands guard over Junction City's selection of desserts (one of which apparently took a hit, as well). (Brian Tombaugh)

Above: The Western theme of Junction City Restaurant is apparent before you ever set foot inside the restaurant. (Brian Tombaugh)

Right: Hiram Mitchell is the man in charge at Junction City – and conductor of the railroad that runs above his head. (Brian Tombaugh)

Hiram has owned Junction City since 1993, and it's become a hangout for the locals as well as the truck drivers passing through. They all enjoy what Hiram calls "the best scenic view of any restaurant on (U.S.) 20" – Junction City looks out over a white-fence-bordered farm. "When the horses get to running," he says, "it's a beautiful thing."

Inside, there's plenty else to hold patrons' attention, all centered around a Western theme. The theme goes from the ceiling (covered with photos of John Wayne and Clint Eastwood) to the walls (covered with relics like a steer skull and a bow-and-arrow set) to the very wall tiles (which sport the occasional painted-on "bullet hole"). A sign outside the kitchen advises: "Cowboys leave your guns at the bar."

Westerns on DVD loop on the TV. Which does Hiram like best? "They're all my favorite," he says of the 1,500 in his collection.

Perhaps the highlight of Junction City is the railroad suspended from the ceiling; Hiram spent 130 hours carefully nailing together all of the individual ties and supports.

As for the food, it's hearty and tasty. Favorites include the biscuits and gravy and the fried bologna ("Drivers love it," Hiram says). There's also the Trucker's Special: two eggs, two slices of bacon, two hotcakes, two links of sausage and taters. They'll even top off a thermos with coffee before a driver starts on the next leg of his haul. All that's left for the departing driver to do is check the clock on the wall to remind himself of the difference between "South Bend time" and "Chicago time."

A reclaimed sign found in the basement is prominently displayed at Jennie Rae's. (Brian Tombaugh)

BOB'S BAR-B-Q, INC. — 18 MILES WEST OF SOUTH BEND, IND.

JUNCTION ROUTES 2 AND 20 — RESTAURANT SEATING 150 PERSONS — SERVING DINNERS AND LUNCHES

Above: Strawberry-stuffed French toast is but one of the decadent breakfast delights to come out of the kitchen at Jennie Rae's. (Brian Tombaugh)

Left: The back of a postcard for Bob's Bar-B-Q (the former resident of Jennie Rae's) advertised it as "71 miles east of Chicago," "175 miles west of Toledo," and "200 miles west of Detroit." (Courtesy Russell Rein)

Jennie Rae's

5201 E. U.S. 20
Rolling Prairie
(574) 778-4100

As with so many other Lincoln Highway sites, Jennie Rae's is not the first to occupy its location. And current owner Jennifer Baltes has taken pains to honor the past.

The previous establishment, Bob's Bar-B-Q, was a 24-hour-a-day landmark topped by a huge Berghoff beer sign for 1940s travelers nearing the intersection of U.S. 20 and State Road 2. Also run

by the proprietors of Bob's was Wiley's Camp, which boasted of "Indiana's finest modern-equipped cabins and restaurant." Among its amenities were a water pump, picnic tables and separate toilets for men and women.

The cabins are long gone from the site, if not from the Bob's Bar-B-Q legacy. Jennifer's in-laws have converted one of them into a chicken coop.

Photos and vintage postcards of Bob's dot the walls at Jennie Rae's. Jennifer – who co-owns her namesake business along with her husband, Jeff – recalls her excitement at finding an old Bob's sign in a downstairs walk-in cooler during renovations in 2005. "I think I may have jumped up and down a few times when we discovered what it said," she says of the sign that now occupies a spot next to the

Above: As it did in its days as Bob's Bar-B-Q, Jennie Rae's offers a welcome rest stop for Lincoln Highway travelers. (Brian Tombaugh)

Pies are a big hit, too – some customers order their dessert even before their meal. "Tells me I'm doing something right," Jennifer says. She adds that one of her regulars buys a pie every Friday to give away. "A pay-it-forward kind of thing," she explains. "He's almost at 300 pies."

SAUSAGE GRAVY
(courtesy of Jennifer Baltes)

1 lb. butter
2 Tbsp. salt
3 cups cooked sausage
Pinch of black pepper
1 Tbsp. onion powder
2 Tbsp. ham base
4 cups flour
3 quarts 2-percent milk

Combine and heat first six ingredients until fully melted and boiling. Add flour and stir until fully combined. It should look like a thick roux. once your roux is hot, add milk, stirring until fully combined. Keep on stove on low heat until gravy thickens to desired consistency.

cash register. "We've been fortunate enough to have great customers who have brought us dishes, matchboxes, an old set of keys from the cabins and tons of postcards. … I can never have enough memorabilia from that era!"

Jennie Rae's calls itself the place "where our family meets yours." The Friday night all-you-can-eat fish fry is especially popular, as are the breakfasts where you can sample some of Jennie Rae's signature homemade jams. A total of 13 fresh-fruit flavors – cherry, blueberry, peach and strawberry among them – are available in take-home jars, as well.

Jennifer cautions: "I can't be too specific as I am a 'pinch of this and a pinch of that' kind of girl!"

Candy Kitchen
705 Lincolnway West
LaPorte

In 1920, James Petros joined the wave of Greek immigrants who made their way to northern Indiana to work in the candy business. LaPorte's Candy Kitchen was already an established family business.

For 10 years James worked, eventually saving the $700 he needed to return to his hometown of Agion, Greece, and find his wife, Panajota. The couple returned to LaPorte, where James eventually ran the shop that advertised "our own ice cream made from pure cream only. We make special high grade chocolates put up in beautiful boxes."

The Candy Kitchen also featured a lunch counter, with sandwiches available for between 10 and 40 cents. There was a special menu featuring "grill-kist

(Courtesy LaPorte County Historical Society)

light lunches." For dessert, the themed sundae options included patriotic ("American Beauty") and romantic ("Tonight You Belong to Me").

California Fruit Company
703 Lincolnway West
LaPorte

The California Fruit Company featured canned goods and nuts and specialized in cold meats, in addition to having bushels of apples and other fruits. Plenty of wicker baskets also were available to shoppers.

(Courtesy LaPorte County Historical Society)

John and Billie Pappas, the J and B of the café, ran the restaurant begun by John's father until the couple's 2014 retirement. (Brian Tombaugh)

B&J's American Cafe occupies a prime location east of the court-house on Lincolnway in downtown LaPorte. (Brian Tombaugh)

B&J's American Cafe

**607 Lincolnway
LaPorte
(219) 362-3474**

The Pappases have retired from B&J's. In May 2015, the restaurant, under the same name, was reopened by new owners Titus and Kimberly Lohr.

During the same week in the mid-1990s, John Pappas was downsized out of his insurance job in Texas and the former tenant left what is now his LaPorte restaurant building. "It was God's way of telling us we needed to change direction," wife Billie says. "That was 15 years and 15,000 plates ago."

B&J's American Cafe carries on a nearly 80-year tradition of dining at the same address along LaPorte's Lincolnway. John's father bought the building from a cousin in 1935; it's been in the family and has been a restaurant ever since.

In many ways, B&J's is a nod to that earlier age. Big band music plays amid classic movie posters and still photos (with some Lincoln Highway memorabilia sprinkled in). A lunch counter runs the length of the dining room. (A period photograph in *The Lincoln Highway across Indiana* shows what was then known as the Lincoln Way Buffet. "The buffet was decorated in the arts and crafts style and provided customers with a fully stocked bar and brass spittoons for spitting convenience," author Jan Shupert-Arick writes.) Other piec-

As you might infer from the name, a nod to Casablanca, B&J's American Cafe is heavy on the movie memorabilia. (Brian Tombaugh)

CHICKEN TETRAZZINI SOUP

(courtesy of Billie Pappas / B&J's American Cafe)

¼ cup margarine
1 cup onion
2 (4 oz.) cans mushrooms, drained
½ cup flour
¼ tsp. pepper
¼ tsp. nutmeg
½ tsp. onion powder
1 cup shredded carrot

2 Tbsp. parsley
1 Tbsp. basil
⅓ cup chicken base
1 cup milk
10 cups water
16 oz. cooked shredded chicken
8 oz. cut up dry spaghetti
1½ cups grated parmesan

In large pot, saute onions and mushrooms in margarine. Next, add flour, pepper, nutmeg, onion powder, carrots, parsley, basil and chicken base. Stir and add milk. Cook to thicken. Add water and shredded chicken. Bring to a boil. Add spaghetti and cook for 10 minutes. Add grated parmesan cheese before placing on steam table.

es of décor were salvaged from elsewhere – signs from downstairs (relics from John's father's American Cafe were found in the basement) and lighting equipment from upstairs (which once housed a portrait studio). A postal window complete with a set of mailboxes is on more or less permanent loan from a friend.

"Our original intent was to restore it for somebody else," John says of the café. But as he spent seven months pulling down the drop ceiling, exposing the long-covered wood paneling and buffing the porcelain tile floor, he felt a familiar pull.

"I've always wanted to run this place," John says, "ever since my dad had it."

Billie (who concedes the restaurant business does allow for "more family togetherness") does the baking. Her treats are available at the front counter. The couple's three sons also have been fixtures at B&J's at various times; each has a menu item named after him.

Above: *Situated on a curve in the road west of downtown LaPorte, the Western Inn attracted many a regular in its day. (Brian Tombaugh)*

Left: *Larry and Leslee Rose tended to the quaint dining room side of the Western Inn; the tavern side sat on the other end from the kitchen. (Brian Tombaugh)*

Western Inn

**610 J Street
LaPorte**

This restaurant – and building – no longer exists. The Western Inn closed in the summer of 2013, ending a 51-year tradition. The contents were auctioned off, and the building was demolished.

You walk up to the Western Inn and hear the sound of dishes clattering in the kitchen, which sits in the center of the building. Enter the yellow-trimmed brick Western Inn from the right, and you're in the bar. Enter from the left to sit in the family-friendly dining room.

Larry Rose's parents, Lawrence and Leavenna Rose, got into the restaurant business in 1963. Larry says at the end of his Marines service in 1965, he was "drafted into it." He took over the Western Inn in 2001; today he runs it with his daughter, Leslee Rose.

Leslee, a restaurant management graduate of Purdue University, is responsible for the dining room's homey touches – the wainscoting created from picket fence panels, wood-cut wall hangings and artificial flowers and plants that give the room a garden feel.

Larry says customers return to the Western Inn for "a little bit of tradition." They're also drawn by the prime rib, steaks and gourmet sandwiches.

Larry says he's not a hobbyist. Since he doesn't golf or fish, "I socialize here," he says.

"We love sassin' each other," he adds. "Rather than a compliment, you get sass."

Larry's civic-mindedness is on display in the signs proclaiming the Western Inn as the meeting place of the Maple City Lions Club. The restaurant also is a participant in LaPorte's annual cruise night.

"We're not a fancy place," says Larry, "just home folks. It's just a good, middle-class, American place."

Pinhook Methodist Church
7353 W. State Route 2
LaPorte

This Greek Revival church already had stood for more than 65 years before the Lincoln Highway came curving past its front door.

The "frame church building was constructed as a one-room, single-story structure … in 1847," according to a National Register of Historic Places nomination form. A cemetery was added three years later; its first burial was James McLung (September 11, 1850), one of two carpenters credited with building Pinhook Methodist Church from hand-hewn walnut logs over a stone foundation.

The church originally served the village of New Durham (later Pinhook). Residents William and Catherine Garwood charged the church $20 for the deed of 0.2 acre of land "to be used as a church forever and ever." Pinhook closed in the early 1900s and stood vacant until 1941, when it reopened as a Sunday school. With the oversight of the Pinhook Mother's Club, the building's interior was refurbished for its 1947 centennial.

That interior features three sections of pew seating (as well as two original walnut pews), a wooden-platform, raised sanctuary separated by a decorative wooden balustrade and a replica pot-belly stove. It has no electricity or plumbing.

The nearly 1,000-grave cemetery now dominates the property, which has grown to nearly 2.5 acres. Veterans of the War of 1812 and the Civil War are buried there, as well as veterans of wars as recent as Afghanistan.

After being abandoned again in 1968, Pinhook was stabilized in 1977 and restored in 1987. The church (added to the National Register in 2009) now hosts weddings, funerals and community activities.

Pinhook Methodist Church has kept watch over travelers since before the time of President Abraham Lincoln, as well as his namesake highway. (Brian Tombaugh)

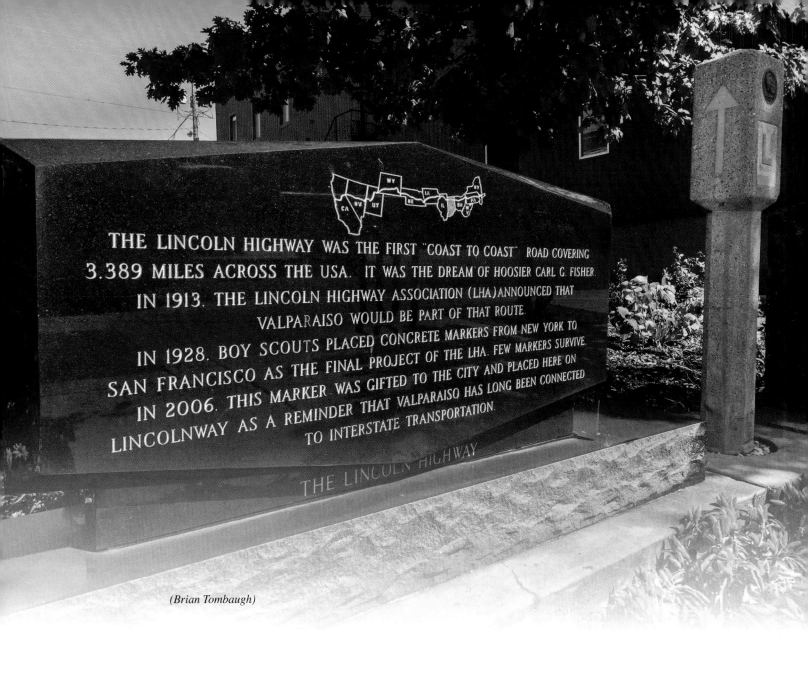

THE LINCOLN HIGHWAY WAS THE FIRST "COAST TO COAST" ROAD COVERING 3,389 MILES ACROSS THE USA. IT WAS THE DREAM OF HOOSIER CARL G. FISHER. IN 1913, THE LINCOLN HIGHWAY ASSOCIATION (LHA) ANNOUNCED THAT VALPARAISO WOULD BE PART OF THAT ROUTE. IN 1928, BOY SCOUTS PLACED CONCRETE MARKERS FROM NEW YORK TO SAN FRANCISCO AS THE FINAL PROJECT OF THE LHA. FEW MARKERS SURVIVE. IN 2006, THIS MARKER WAS GIFTED TO THE CITY AND PLACED HERE ON LINCOLNWAY AS A REMINDER THAT VALPARAISO HAS LONG BEEN CONNECTED TO INTERSTATE TRANSPORTATION.

THE LINCOLN HIGHWAY

(Brian Tombaugh)

Orville Redenbacher got his start in Valparaiso, where the Popcorn Festival every September draws as many as 70,000 people to the city of 31,000 in a single day. Valparaiso also pays homage to its Lincoln Highway heritage with a prominent granite monument and concrete marker outside city hall on Lincolnway downtown.

Porter
COUNTY

(Brian Tombaugh)

OLGA'S PLACE

COAST TO COAST

Olga's
Place
PIZZA & RESTAURANT
EUROPEAN DINING
219-785-7100

Olga's Place
454 Main Street
Westville
(219) 785-7100

The Pecanac family brings a world – or at least a continent – of experience to Olga's Place. Esada Pecanac completed culinary school in Croatia and worked as a chef in Vienna, but she is fond of saying, "Westville is my destiny." That's where she chose to open the restaurant named in honor of her daughter.

The Pecanacs arrived in America in 1994 as they escaped the Yugoslavian civil war. As they tell the story on the Olga's Place website, they sought to give their daughter "a better life, education and freedom."

"We didn't choose to come to the United States; the United States chose us," adds Esada of the family's being selected in an immigration lottery. The Pecanacs made their way to Valparaiso, where a sister of Esada's husband, Ilija, lived. Esada spoke no English; she took jobs cleaning houses and washing dishes while she learned. The family bought a house in Westville, and every day on her way to work, Esada passed the building that would one day become her restaurant.

That building had seen uses as diverse as a railroad station, a fire station and a Ford dealership. Ilija, an electrical engineer by trade, spent 14 months renovating the building. The Pecanacs opened their restaurant in November 2007.

Olga's Place bears little resemblance to any of its past uses. A round, brick pizza oven faces the main dining room. European-style pizzas – named after European cities – are a specialty. (The menu describes Olga's as "a

LAMB SERVED WITH WILD RASPBERRY SAUCE
(courtesy of Esada Pecanac)

11 lb. lamb	For the sauce:	
Salt	1 Tbsp. butter	Season the lamb well with salt, pepper and garlic. Bake for one hour (keep an eye on it).
Pepper	2 Tbsp. oil	
Garlic	1 onion	
	3 Tbsp. brown sugar	
	Garlic	*Sauce:* In butter and oil, fry onions 3-4 minutes. Add brown sugar and fry until caramelized. Add garlic, mint leaves, salt, pepper, raspberries and strawberries. Add a few spoonfuls of the fat liquid from the lamb, plus the balsamic vinegar. Let boil for 2-4 minutes.
	Mint leaves	
	Salt	
	Pepper	
	½-1 cup raspberries	
	7 strawberries, sliced	
	3 Tbsp. balsamic vinegar	

Esada and Olga Pecanac pose before the brick oven that produces so many of the signature dishes of Olga's Place. (Brian Tombaugh)

short drive to a European getaway.") Start your meal with a ramekin of Esada's butternut squash soup – it's like liquid pumpkin pie with a dollop of cream on top. Desserts also span the European map. There are crepes, apple strudel and baklava. "My cooking is still scratch and homemade because I'm old-fashioned," Esada says. All the menu items come from her recipes.

Esada's sense of place even extends to the Lincoln funeral train sign in the field next to Olga's Place. (A similar sign can be found in Wanatah.) She's taken it upon herself to plant and tend to the flowers at the site.

OUT OF THE PAST

Barboul's
U.S. 30 and Indiana 49
Valparaiso

The restaurant first known as Barboul's went through a number of incarnations throughout its life between the late 1930s and the mid-1990s: Marie's Restaurant, The Orange Bowl and Kelsey's Steakhouse. The location also served as the Valparaiso stop for Greyhound buses. The property now is owned by Valparaiso University, and the building was razed as part of the vision for a new entrance to the VU campus.

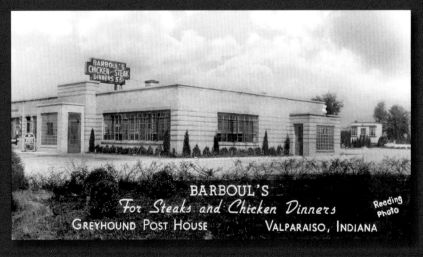

(Courtesy Russell Rein)

OUT OF THE PAST

Strongbow Inn
2405 U.S. 30
Valparaiso

The history of the Strongbow Inn is inextricably tied to that of the Lincoln Highway. The restaurant opened as the rerouted U.S. 30 made its way to Valparaiso in 1940; expansion of the highway and its surroundings shaped the Strongbow for more than 70 years.

The Strongbow (named for a Potawatomi Indian chief) was the vision of Bess Russell Thrun. It was an outgrowth of the Depression-era turkey farm she ran with her husband and a family friend. From the original 28-seat diner, the inn grew to include a bakery and a 500-seat banquet facility.

Former owner Caroline "Chuggie" Adams recalls that "the highway went right through the middle of the farm," and turkeys occasionally had to be herded across the highway so they could find new places to forage for food. "The police did come out and stop what traffic there was," she says.

For the first few years of its existence, Caroline says the Strongbow closed for the winter – "because they didn't clear the highway." (World War II-era gas rationing was another factor.) The restaurant would reopen on the third Thursday in March. Summer was es-pecially busy, as Strongbow was a welcome stop for those who had escaped for the weekend to their lake homes. "On Sunday night, you could hardly close," Caroline recalls.

Thanksgiving always held special significance for a restaurant that specialized in turkey. Caroline's son Russ Adams, who assumed ownership of the Strongbow in 1993, recalls that during the Tuesday of Thanksgiving week through Thursday, the restaurant would go through 11,000 pounds

THE WORLD'S BEST BUTTERED PECANS
(courtesy of Caroline Adams; reprinted from Dinner at Chuggie's)

A family favorite. Buttered pecans are perfect plain, on salads or with ice cream.

¼ cup butter, melted
6 cups pecans
Salt

Coat pecans in melted butter. Lay on baking sheet, and sprinkle with salt. Bake at 300 degrees, turning every 10 minutes. This might take an hour or more. Taste one to see. (They should be crisp, not chewy.)

Put a few cups of buttered pecans in decorative bags and give them to family for Christmas gifts.

Both images: Enlarged photos on walls around the Strongbow Inn showed snapshots of life on the turkey farm, as well as at the venerated Valparaiso restaurant. (Brian Tombaugh)

of its signature meat. Russ, a Culinary Institute of America graduate, also has served as Strongbow's head chef. He is quick to point out that other entrees were popular as well – from steaks to the Friday perch special.

In 2013, the Adamses sold the Strongbow to another area-based and family-based company. The Luke Co. has maintained the inn for Sunday and holiday brunches as well as banquets, but full restaurant service and the adjoining bakery were closed in March 2015.

Right: Many of Strongbow Inn's savory entrees and starters, even the chili, were turkey-based. (Brian Tombaugh)

STRONGBOW TURKEY PIE

(courtesy of Caroline Adams; reprinted from Dinner at Chuggie's)

This recipe dates back to the earliest days of Strongbow, more than sixty years ago, when Mother was developing recipes that have come to be known across the country as signature dishes at Strongbow. Literally thousands are served and sold every year. Makes 4 pies.

Dough:
    2 cups all-purpose flour
    ½ tsp. salt
    ⅔ cup shortening or lard
    6-7 Tbsp. cold water

Filling:
    4 Tbsp. butter
    ½ cup chopped onion
    1 cup sliced celery
    3 Tbsp. flour
    2 cups hot turkey broth
    ⅛ tsp. poultry seasoning
    3 cups cubed turkey

Gravy:
    4 Tbsp. butter
    ¼ cup flour
    2 cups turkey broth
    ½ tsp. salt

In bowl, stir together 2 cups flour and ½ teaspoon salt. Cut in shortening until pieces are the size of small peas. Sprinkle 1 tablespoon of the water over part of the mixture and toss gently. Push to side of bowl. Repeat until all is moistened.

Form dough into a ball. On a lightly floured surface, flatten dough. Roll to ⅛-inch thickness. Cut into four 4-inch-diameter circles and four 6-inch-diameter circles.

Melt butter in medium skillet, add onion and celery, and saute until transparent. Add flour, stirring constantly, and cook until bubbly. Now add broth and seasonings, stirring and cooking for several minutes until thick. Add turkey. Cool.

Place 6-inch round of dough in a small dish to shape the pie. Place turkey mixture in this and cover with the smaller 4-inch round of dough. Moisten edges and bring up the edges of lower dough, crimping over top layer. (The smaller layer will be on the bottom for baking, the 6-inch round will be on top, nice and smooth.) Before baking, poke a hole in the middle of the top.

Place the pies on a lightly greased cookie sheet. Bake in 425-degree oven for about 25 minutes or until light brown. Serve with gravy.

To make gravy: Melt butter, blend in flour, and gradually add broth and salt until a nice, thick gravy results. Serve over individual turkey pies with cranberry sauce.

(If you don't have time to make your own pie crust, you can use store-bought. Just be sure you have enough crust for a 10-inch pie. Roll the dough and cut four 6-inch rounds and four 4-inch rounds.)

Two stuffed lions behind glass and mounted animal heads (buffalo, deer, etc.) are part of the decor at Tony's Place. (Brian Tombaugh)

Tony's Place

**218 Lincolnway
Valparaiso
(219) 464-1018**

There are basically only two rules at Tony's Place: Come hungry, and bring cash. It's been that way for more than half a century.

"We've been hangin' in for 57 years," says second-generation owner Tony Gengo. His father (also Tony, "Pop" to his son) started with a 20-seat takeout restaurant, Valparaiso's first pizzeria, atop the Lincolnway Hill in 1955. Tony's moved a quarter mile west in 1962 and, a few years later, expanded into the store next door.

"It was standing room only for years and years and years because we were the only ones here," recalls Tammie Charnas, a waitress for more than 30 years.

The younger Tony took it upon himself to expand again in the 1970s while his parents were away on a Florida vacation. They returned to a restaurant that seated up to 300 people.

Many of those customers come back today for a taste of what they remember from growing up. And it's Tony's mission to make sure the experience is just as they remember it – from the food to the décor.

"They like that nothing's changed," Tony says. "We do exactly what we did 50 years ago."

In truth, it's been even longer than that. Many of the recipes made their way to America with the Gengo family from Naples, Italy, late in the 19th century. Tony's ancestors arrived in New York City and opened a bakery – among the first in the United States to offer prepackaged macaroni for sale. That bakery remains open today in the city's Fordham neighborhood.

Tony is particularly proud of his food preparation. "Everything's baked here. We've never had a fryer." They've also never seen the need to take credit cards – a policy that served Tony's well during a power outage. Customers ate by candlelight as their food came out of the gas-fired ovens.

Pop's Marinara Sauce, available by the quart, is prepared fresh daily from Tony's secret recipe and advertised as all natural with no preservatives. (Brian Tombaugh)

Tammie, somewhat immodestly, says quality is the key to Tony's success. "It's the best pizza on the planet," she says. "The crust is unbelievable.

"You can't help but get hooked on it."

And whether you get hooked on it or not, at some point you'll want to try one of the cheekily named pasta dishes, such as the "Fungus Among Us" spaghetti with mushroom sauce.

Restaurante don Quijote

119 E. Lincolnway
Valparaiso
(219) 462-7976

The giant paella pan in the window is emblematic of the message Carlos Rivero wants everyone to understand: His cuisine is Spanish, not Mexican. Specifically, his recipes can be traced to his family in northern Spain. "I decided I was going to be true to my roots," Carlos says of the restaurant he opened in 1985. "You have to be true to yourself."

Carlos' roots are in his native Spain, where he was a restaurateur before coming to the United States in 1978 (his wife is from Merrillville). He came for love; he stayed for the hunting and fishing ("I think it was the Lake Michigan water") while earning a living in the region's steel mills. "Some part of my life was missing," he says of his inability to hunt in his native land. Carlos returns to Europe as often as his busy schedule allows, sometimes as leader of a tour group. "Spain is a country with so much to offer," he says. "I get over there and my eyes just go crazy," he adds of its food.

But Carlos also has found plenty to keep him busy in Valparaiso, where he is involved with issues such as homelessness. "I decided from the first moment that I was going to be involved in my community," he says, adding, "My wife says I should retire just to go to meetings. I want to be everywhere – that's my problem."

Below: Don Quijote's Spanish flair adds to the culinary diversity of Lincolnway through downtown Valparaiso. (Brian Tombaugh)

Carlos' business partner, Elena Jambrina, is also from Spain; she began as Don Quijote's dessert chef. Their business is in a building that had been a French restaurant and a sporting goods store in previous incarnations, but it was built as a slaughterhouse. A terra cotta overhang adds to Don Quijote's Spanish flair.

Carlos originally planned to call his restaurant La Sangria. But he opted instead to name it for the nomadic hero of Spain's best-known literary classic ("It was an adventure to come," Carlos says). A Don Quijote mural dominates the back wall of the main dining room. The entryway showcases a variety of imported meats, cheeses and packaged foods; you can do additional shopping at Don Quijote's Spanish imports store next door. A variety of pans hangs from a rack in the front window, but the huge paella pan is the one that inevitably catches your eye; it can feed Spain's national dish (Carlos says his version of the saffron rice-based dish "looks beautiful and tastes good") to as many as 160 people.

Below: Elena Jambrina and Carlos Rivero have brought the taste of their native Spain to Indiana and become renowned throughout the region. (Brian Tombaugh)

Old Style Inn

5 Lincolnway
Valparaiso
(219) 462-5600

The Old Style Inn has operated continuously along the Lincoln Highway since 1932. Since November 2000, the Old Style has been owned and operated by Mary and Kenn Grcich.

"It has always been my passion and my love," says Mary of the Old Style. "I still can't wait to get here every day." She had waitressed at the inn in three separate stints before the opportunity arose to buy it.

Mary says she and her husband never considered changing the name. "We felt that's what we were buying."

The inn is a family – and friends – affair. Most of Mary's employees have been with her for at least 10 years. Husband Kenn does as much maintenance as he can, and Mary's son Bruce often is behind the bar.

The decorating also reflects Mary's style. It's apparent she's a Beatles fan. Posters, photos, plates and other memorabilia line the walls. And twice a year, the Old Style hosts a Beatles night. "I never dreamt

Below: A bar encompasses the west wall of Old Style Inn's front half, so patrons must be at least 18 years old. There, they can enjoy food such as the double-stuffed potato with cheddar cheese, mushrooms and slices of filet mignon. (Brian Tombaugh)

it would be so successful," Mary says. Other annual celebrations include Valentine's Day, St. Patrick's Day and Tropical Night on June 21 (the first day of summer).

Downtown Valparaiso has seen an explosion of restaurants in recent years – it went from five to 12 in just the first 13 years of the Grciches' Old Style ownership. Mary believes she offers something unique among all the ethnic options.

"I still think we're the best buck on the block," she says. "We need comfort food downtown – and I'm the place for comfort food." That includes the Old Style's top three sellers: prime rib, lake perch and filet mignon.

Indiana native Henry C. Ostermann served as vice president and field secretary of the Lincoln Highway Association. He was killed in an accident along the highway in Iowa in 1920. Landscape architect Jens Jensen was hired in 1926 to design a memorial in Ostermann's honor. The bench he crafted remains along the Lincoln Highway between Schererville and Dyer, in front of land occupied by the palatial residence known as Meyer's Castle. The memorial was placed along a stretch of highway known as the "ideal section," where the pavement, lighting and bridges were meant to serve as a model for state-of-the-art construction techniques.

Lake
COUNTY

Deep River County Park

9410 Old Lincoln Highway
Hobart
(219) 947-1958

John Wood arrived in the wilds that are now Lake County, Indiana, in 1835. Two years later, he retrieved his family from his hometown of Danvers, Massachusetts, and brought them to the plot of land he had bought for $1,000 from a Potawatomi Indian chief. He built a sawmill on the banks of the Deep River. The grist mill he added in 1838 has become a focal point of a 1,200-acre park.

The wood-frame structure was upgraded to brick by John's son, Nathan, in 1876. That building was added to the National Register of Historic Places in 1975. The nomination form describes how "by 1954, all of the machinery and conveyor belts had been stripped from the mill." The building was renovated in 1976; corn meal is still ground by the millstones today.

Also on the park grounds are miles of hiking trails, a gazebo and Grinder Field, home of the Deep River Grinders vintage baseball team. The sign welcoming you to the field says: "Upon this field the game is played according to the original 33 rules of baseball adopted in 1858."

With John Wood's mill as a backdrop, the grounds of Deep River County Park – including its large gazebo – are a popular spot for outdoor weddings. (Brian Tombaugh)

Albanese Confectionery

5441 East Lincoln Highway
Merrillville
(855) 272-3227

Albanese Confectionery, just south of the old Lincoln Highway route, makes for a mouth-watering and worthwhile side trip. Gummi bears are a specialty, but the company's wide range of candies is likely to satisfy even the most finicky sweet tooth.

Albanese has been in the candy business since 1983. Gummis became a focus in 1997, when the company went online with a new manufacturing plant in Hobart. On its website, Albanese cites itself as an "innovative candy company" that has unlocked secrets allowing for better flavor release and more intense flavor for its sour gummis. Albanese has developed a gummi that does not freeze (so it can be used to flavor ice cream) and is in the process of developing gummi medicines.

Free factory tours are available. But the website cautions: "From November (to) December and March (to) April, no tours will be given. Santa and the Easter Bunny visit us every year during that time."

(Brian Tombaugh)

Teibel's

U.S. 30 and U.S. 41
Schererville
(219) 865-2000

Chicken and perch draw diners to Teibel's from near and far. Family hospitality keeps them coming back.

Paul Teibel is the latest to carry on the four-generation tradition; Paul's great grandfather Martin, along with Martin's brother Stephen, opened the original 12-seat diner in 1929. "As word spread from coast to coast along 30 and 41," a history on the restaurant's website says, "Teibel's family restaurant grew into a Midwest tradition."

Today, Teibel's main dining room sits on land once occupied by the original diner, seen here in a 1929 postcard. (Courtesy Schererville Historical Society)

of perch and 600 to 700 pounds of chicken. The chicken is prepared using the same recipe that accompanied the original Teibel family when they emigrated from Austria.

In the course of a conversation, Paul is likely to return several times to the same theme: "We work hard, but we have a lot of fun doing it." That fun is especially evident in December, when everybody pitches in to put up the Christmas decorations (including the two men who spend three full weeks getting the outside lights just right). "We deck the halls," Paul says. "Even in the kitchen – some (decorations) make it in there."

Paul is currently the only Teibel working at his namesake restaurant. "It's the first time that's ever happened," he says. Paul's father, Steve, worked at Teibel's for 40 years and still makes the occasional appearance. And even though he has a degree in hospitality, Paul says, "I learned everything from my dad. He's the best teacher I ever had."

Paul describes the dining room as "the middle of the doughnut," with Teibel's various other seating options surrounding it. There are three banquet rooms that can accommodate up to 400 people, a lounge and a coffee shop.

The banquet rooms make Teibel's a popular destination around northwest Indiana for wedding receptions, baby showers and class reunions. "You never know what you're going to get on a Saturday," Paul says.

Foodwise, though, you always know what you're going to get. In a typical week, Paul estimates, Teibel's goes through 1,000 pounds

Meyer's Castle

**1370 Joliet Street
Dyer
(219) 865-8452**

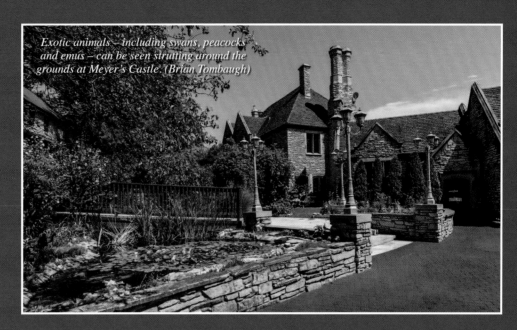

Exotic animals – including swans, peacocks and emus – can be seen strutting around the grounds at Meyer's Castle. (Brian Tombaugh)

This Jacobethan Revival classic is not visible from the Lincoln Highway, but it commands a spot atop 10 acres of the highest land in the area.

The castle was built between 1929 and 1931 for Joseph Ernest Meyer, who became a millionaire through his cultivation, sale and promotion of herbal medicines. He also was involved in banking.

Joseph hired architect Cosbey Bernard, Sr. to design the stone mansion Joseph envisioned as a replica of a Scottish castle he had once seen. Stairways, trim and other ornamentation were of Indiana limestone. Inside, the three-story residence featured carved-oak paneling and details including rosettes, griffins, serpent and leaves, finished over the course of two years by European craftsmen. A 400-pound brass chandelier dominated the grand entrance hall.

The castle's terraced grounds included stone windmills, sunken rock gardens, a gazebo, a goldfish pond, a bird sanctuary and orchards.

Joseph lived in the home until his death in 1950; the property was sold by his survivors to developers in 1975. The castle now hosts special events and is home to Rodizio, an Argentinian steakhouse.

OUT OF THE PAST

Burson's Drug Store
Dyer

Burson's Drug Store in Dyer featured all the soda fountain attractions of its day – Coca-Cola products, Planters nuts, and Borden's chocolate, vanilla and strawberry ice cream for 20 cents a pint. The Mickey Mouse decorations above the soda fountain give some hint as to the era of this photo.

(Courtesy Lake County Museum)

Foodie's Marketcafé

151 Joliet Street
Dyer
(219) 864-3030

Cathy Cameron's vision of her business is that of a "comfortable place for people to come during the day." Red vinyl chairs and black-and-white-checked tablecloths add to the diner vibe, while a fireplace and wooden peg games encourage you to linger over your made-while-you-wait food. Or you might grab a magazine from the rack by the door as you enter.

Foodie's serves what Cathy – who co-owns the business with her husband, Tim – calls "mom food."

"It's a multitude of things I've always made," she says. There are reuben, pulled pork and meatloaf-melt sandwiches, and there are plenty of vegetarian options as well. As for soups, you can choose from among many; "steak and ale" is the top seller.

Foodie's website invites customers to come in and say hello to the "bread lady." Cathy, a former bread salesperson, decided to start Foodie's featuring the bread she already sold. (Anything on a pretzel-bread roll is a particularly good choice, she notes.) "I knew one (good) thing would lead to another," Cathy says.

Bread and other baked goods figure prominently in the market portion of Foodie's, as do pastas, spices and sauces, plus wines and craft-brewed beers.

As they look around Foodie's, customers can catch glimpses of Dyer history. Cathy has many framed photos of Dyer's growing days as a railroad town. The marketcafé and a pizzeria that shares the building sit on the site of a former bank whose corner location made it a frequent target of robbers.

FOODIE'S CHILI

(courtesy of Cathy Cameron)

1 lb. ground beef
1 lb. pork sausage (hot or mild)
¼ cup butter (½ stick)
2 yellow onions, chopped
1 bell pepper, chopped
1 banana pepper (if you want a little heat)
      or 1 red pepper, chopped
2 Tbsp. chili powder
1 Tbsp. chopped or minced garlic
1 tsp. celery salt

1 Tbsp. salt
1 tsp. ground black pepper
1 16-oz. can of black beans or pinto beans
1 28-oz. can of crushed tomatoes
1 28-oz. can (or 2 smaller) petite diced tomatoes
1 6-oz. can of tomato paste
¼ cup red wine vinegar
2 tsp. Worcestershire sauce
1 tsp. hot sauce, or to taste
½ cup of water

Brown both meats in a large stockpot over medium-high heat until no longer pink. Drain meat in colander but leave about 5 Tbsp. of the drippings in the pot. Melt the butter in the pot with the drippings. Add the onions, peppers, chili powder, garlic, celery salt, salt and black pepper. Sauté until vegetables are tender. Add meat back to pot. Add the beans, crushed tomatoes, diced tomatoes, tomato paste, red wine vinegar, Worcestershire sauce, hot sauce and water. Stir and bring to a boil. Reduce heat and simmer uncovered for about 30 minutes until the flavors are well-blended and the chili is slightly thickened. Stir frequently to prevent sticking.

Tip: Use a food processor to chop the onions and peppers all at one time. … Don't forget the love!

Both images: *Cathy Cameron's Foodie's Marketcafé combines all the best elements of a diner with the shopping experience of a specialty grocery. (Brian Tombaugh)*

Lincolnway Auto, on the eastern edge of Plymouth, reflects owner Cecil Wilson's love of vintage cars – from the classic Chevy Malibu sitting in the showroom to the passing hot rod that's reflected in the window. (Brian Tombaugh)

SOUTHERN ROUTE

By 1928, the original route of the Lincoln Highway had been refined and somewhat shortened. With that in mind, we return east to pick up that shorter route on the western outskirts of Fort Wayne.

The Lincolndale Drive-In on Fort Wayne's Goshen Road had a capacity of 500 vehicles; it closed in 1982 and has been demolished.

Allen
COUNTY

Lake Township School No. 4

10707 W. Washington Center Road
Fort Wayne

The book *100 Years with Arcola 1866-1966* describes this building as "the center school and township house." It was built in 1878 at a cost of roughly $800 and served as a schoolhouse for nearly the first 40 years of its existence. A plaque on the building's east wall credits its construction to "Wm. Goheen (an Allen County farmer and deed holder to the school site) & Trust."

"In 1920 a movement began for a new elementary and high school," the book continues, with "the new school (beginning) its career in September 1922."

The former school and community center has since become the home of Chris and Sonia Welch; it has been a residence since at least the mid-1950s. Chris' grandfather has shared tales that the building also has served functions from a restaurant to a square dance hall to a brothel. The Welches and their children have lived in the property, one of only a few historic two-story brick schoolhouses still standing, since 1987.

The Welches are happy to share the history of their home as they sit in their cozy kitchen, decorated with vintage cast-iron skillets, egg beaters and bottles. The smell of burning wood drifts through the air; the wood-fired stove heats the house well enough that the Welches are comfortable in jeans and T-shirts, even in mid-winter.

Sonia and Chris Welch's converted-schoolhouse home has seen many other functions in its near century and a half of existence. (Brian Tombaugh)

Simply returning school No. 4 to livable condition took plenty of vision – the basement had three feet of standing water when the Welches first viewed it. And while the attic was insulated, the walls were not. As with any 134-year-old building, the home continues to do its share of settling. For instance, the building's original lath occasionally comes loose above one of the home's drop ceilings. "Every now and then, you can hear something drop," Chris says. The downspouts and mortaring also have required particular attention.

But the craftsmanship is undeniable. "It's a pretty tight house, no doubt about it," Chris says.

The renovation process yielded its share of treasures. Chris describes finding old ink jars in the area that is now the home's front porch, as well as a military knife out in the yard. The Welches also have hosted a visitor whose mother had been a student at the school.

Occasionally, the curiosity to discover what lies beneath gets the best of the Welches; they've torn up a few floors but have so far resisted the temptation to tap into their home's walls. Chris admits, though, he's "always thinking about that."

ENCHILADA SOUP

(courtesy of Sonia Welch)

2 lb. chicken breast, cut into small pieces
1 medium onion (diced)
2 large cans Hunt's diced tomatoes
24 oz. enchilada sauce
4 oz. can green chiles
1 tsp. minced garlic
1 cup water
2 14-oz. cans chicken broth OR 4 chicken bouillon cubes
3 tsp. cumin
1 tsp. chili powder
15-oz. can kidney beans OR black beans
10 oz. frozen corn
1 Tbsp. cilantro

Cook chicken and onions together until chicken is fully cooked. Add remaining ingredients. Let simmer for 45 minutes to an hour.

To serve: Pour into a bowl, then add shredded taco cheese and tortilla chips.

OUT OF THE PAST

Hilger's Farm Market and Hilger's Farm Restaurant

13210 U.S. 30 West
Fort Wayne

The Hilger family's "labor of love" has been lauded by radio personality Paul Harvey and even President Ronald Reagan. While their restaurant is closed now, the Hilger family farm continues to be a thriving 21st century operation (you can follow them on Facebook).

That's a far cry from the days of 1925, when Henry Hilger took his horse-drawn carriage door to door in Fort Wayne, peddling onions and carrots (he later upgraded to a Model T). In 1973, his sons John and Joe Hilger opened a farm market at 13210 U.S. 30 W.; it featured that same Hilger-grown produce, as well as locally produced baked goods and cheeses. According to Henry Hilger's Fort Wayne *News-Sentinel* obituary: "The farm market began with peas and corn. Eventually, several other vegetables and strawberries were added, and Hilger's became a popular 'pick-your-own' site."

John Hilger shows off one of the many pumpkins in a Hilgers' Farm field between the old Lincoln Highway and U.S. 30 in western Allen County. (Brian Tombaugh)

Joe and Elaine Hilger stand in front of a barn on land farmed by the Hilger family for nearly a century. (Brian Tombaugh)

In 1987, the Hilgers branched out, opting to carry over the farm theme by placing their restaurant in a building built to look like an old farm. At its peak, the restaurant employed up to 350 people, many of them in their first job.

"We educated many, many teenagers to the workforce," John Hilger says, adding that a fair number of those employees dated one another; some even married. "We were better at that than serving food," he jokes.

Hilger's Farm Restaurant featured a banquet hall on its second level and hosted company picnics in addition to serving restaurant patrons. John says his satisfaction came in seeing his customers satisfied. "I enjoy watching people enjoy what you put in front of them," he says.

Among the restaurant's specialties was its mashed potatoes – "We're one of the biggest potato growers in the state," John says – loaded with cream, butter, garlic, salt and pepper. The barbecue sauce perfected by Hilger's parents was also a big hit with diners.

The picturesque setting was the launching spot for campaigns by a number of Hoosier politicians, with Richard Lugar, Dan Quayle and Dan Coats among them. At harvest time, Hilger's Fall Pumpkin Festival drew families to attractions including hayrides, a straw maze and pyramid, and plenty of rides.

Hilger's Farm Restaurant closed in 2006, but produce still is available at a family farm stand just off U.S. 30.

GRANDMOTHER MARY'S STRAWBERRY SPONGE CAKE
(courtesy of John Hilger and The News-Sentinel archives)

1½ cups cake flour
1½ tsp. baking powder
½ tsp. salt
6 eggs
1 cup plus 2 Tbsp. sugar
1 tsp. vanilla
¼ tsp. lemon juice
1 quart washed and mashed strawberries, mixed with 1 cup sugar
Whipped cream

Prepare two 9-inch layer pans by greasing bottom only and lining with waxed paper. Do not grease sides.

Sift flour, baking powder and salt together and set aside. Beat 6 eggs until foamy and add 1 cup plus 2 Tbsp. sugar. Beat egg and sugar mixture until it stands in soft peaks (about 15 minutes). Fold in vanilla and lemon juice. Fold in dry ingredients and pour into prepared pans. Bake at 425 degrees for 15 minutes or until inserted knife comes out clean.

Cool 5 minutes, then run a knife around the edge of pan and remove cake. Cut into two halves horizontally. Turn cut side up and pour on mashed strawberry-sugar mixture. Top with second half of cake, cut side up, and more strawberries. Repeat process with second cake, creating a four-layer cake with strawberries in between. Top with whipped cream. Slice in wedges to serve.

(Brian Tombaugh)

Although in many places the original route of the Lincoln Highway has been obscured or abandoned, its influence can still be found. On the western edge of Columbia City, the Lincoln Estates subdivision, with its Emancipation Court, is a typical example.

Whitley
COUNTY

OUT OF THE PAST

30 Club
501 E. Chicago Street
Columbia City

For 30 years, the 30 Club was a destination spot, both in Columbia City and for miles around. Dave Johnston, proprietor of The Nook in Columbia City, recalls the "high-end meals" the supper club featured. "It looked great every time you went in."

In 1945, Richard and Sara Stahlhut took over Cleland's Service Station and Lunch Room; by August 1946, renovations were complete and the 30 Club was open. The Stahlhuts spelled out their philosophy on the first page of the club's oversized menu. One of those menus, believed to date to the mid-1950s, was part of a cache of 30 Club memorabilia discovered in 2011.

"In this house are served the finest people in the world … our patrons. Good words of pleasant patrons have made the '30' Club one of the most popular eating places in Northern Indiana. … Therefore we extend to you our sincere apprecia-

tion for your past and future patronage. We will continue to maintain this establishment, a restaurant of distinction, with a unique and pleasant atmosphere which we hope will please you in the future. … You are invited to inspect our kitchen at any time."

The menu featured steaks at prices from $2.50 to $3.50, as well as seafood entrees (lobster tail, $2.25), wines and liqueurs, and "late evening suggestions" (chop suey/chow mein, $.85).

In 1974, the Stahlhuts sold the 30 Club to Don Lomont; his ownership was to last less than two years. One night in June 1974, Don left the restaurant (and the apartment he kept on the second floor) about 11:20 p.m. for Fort Wayne. An hour later, his manager closed the club for the night. An hour after that, the building was reported on fire. The loss was total and was estimated at $200,000. The fire was believed to have started accidentally behind a piece of machinery in the basement.

Now on the site is a Masonic lodge. Parking lot repair work in 2011 uncovered the menu, now part of the collection of the Whitley County Historical Society.

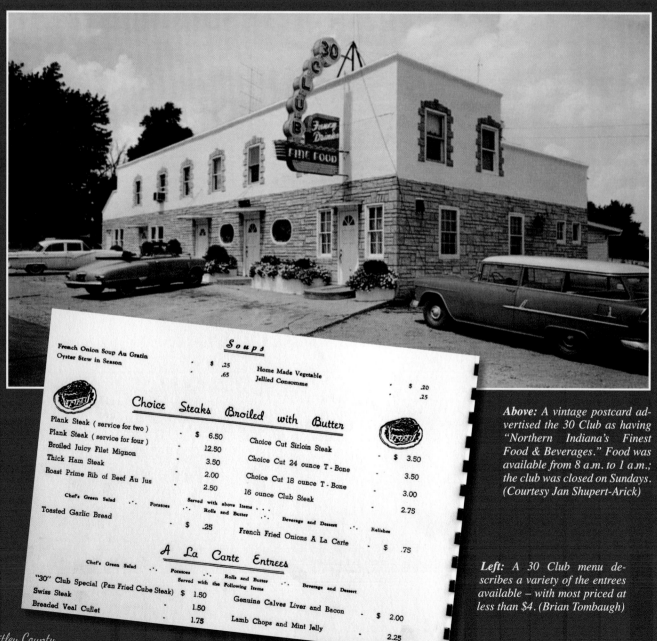

Above: A vintage postcard advertised the 30 Club as having "Northern Indiana's Finest Food & Beverages." Food was available from 8 a.m. to 1 a.m.; the club was closed on Sundays. (Courtesy Jan Shupert-Arick)

Left: A 30 Club menu describes a variety of the entrees available – with most priced at less than $4. (Brian Tombaugh)

Thomas Marshall House
(Whitley County Historical Museum)

108 W. Jefferson Street
Columbia City
(260) 244-6372

Two blocks north of where the Lincoln Highway cuts through Columbia City sits the home of the 28th vice president. Thomas Riley Marshall served with Woodrow Wilson from 1913 to 1921. The Democrat also had one term as Indiana's governor from 1909 to 1913. He is best remembered as the source of the quip, "What this country needs is a good five-cent cigar."

Marshall was born in North Manchester, Indiana, in 1854. In 1874, the attorney moved into the Columbia City home he would occupy until leaving for Indianapolis

after his election in 1908. That home now serves as a tribute to Marshall's memory, as well as the repository of Whitley County history.

Period pieces fill the home – with many serving as display areas. The dining room is filled with the furniture believed to have been used by the Marshall family itself. The round table (with leaves that increase its size to 10 feet), six chairs, sideboard and buffet were acquired at an estate sale after having been passed out of the Marshall family's hands.

FRIED OYSTERS
(courtesy of Dani Tippmann, Whitley County Historical Society)

"For one dozen and a half oysters, there will be required two eggs, one-fourth teaspoonful of pepper, one level tablespoonful of salt and one pint of crumbs; use one-half the salt and pepper to season the oysters and the rest to season the crumbs. Spread the oysters on a towel to drain; after seasoning them with salt and pepper, roll them in fine, dry bread or cracker crumbs; dip them in beaten egg and again roll in plenty of crumbs; have lard about four inches deep in frying kettle, and when it is so hot that blue smoke arises from the center, cover the bottom of the frying basket with a single layer of oysters, plunge into the fat, cook one minute and a half, drain and serve immediately. ...(Two tablespoonsful) of tomato catsup may be mixed with the eggs. Remember that there are few things that require the fat so hot as oysters or that spoil so quickly if allowed to stand after frying."

– Mrs. Thomas R. Marshall,
The Presbyterian Cook Book

Both images: In 1915, Vice President Thomas Marshall returned to his home state to take part in dedication ceremonies for the newly completed Lincoln Highway. (Brian Tombaugh)

on New York's Coney Island that dominates the east wall. The "big ol' blank wall" of the 12-foot-wide Nook was abandoned by the first artist who tried to fill it; his successor (who had "never been to an amusement park in his life," Dave says) spent nearly three months finishing the job. The mural, a Nook fixture since 1982, will remain one for the foreseeable future. "There's a lot of things there to look at," Dave says. "Our customers would miss it."

Above: Hot dogs and a pot of chili sit on the grill at The Nook, waiting to be served up as one of the restaurant's signature dishes. (Brian Tombaugh)

The Nook

223 W. Van Buren Street
Columbia City
(260) 248-8700

Owner Dave Johnston figures The Nook is nearing its 3 millionth hot dog sold; somebody figured out that if they were laid end to end, they would stretch from Columbia City to South Bend.

Dave opened The Nook in July 1971 after nine years working at another restaurant in town. At the beginning, his restaurant served only 15 customers at a time, but Dave saw the need to expand after his first couple of years. "We've never had a problem keeping it filled," he says.

The Nook is a family-run business. Dave's daughter-in-law runs the restaurant these days; her sister and Dave's granddaughter also work there.

The menu is "pretty basic," Dave says. "It's the same as it was in years past." You can get burgers or breaded tenderloins ("Some people never eat a hot dog in here"), but he says The Nook goes through eight times as many hot dog buns as round buns for its other sandwiches. Many of those hot dogs are topped off with The Nook's signature homemade coney sauce.

While enjoying their meals, diners also can admire the huge mural based

Dave Johnston's restaurant is in its fifth decade as a favored hangout in downtown Columbia City. (Brian Tombaugh)

(Brian Tombaugh)

Warsaw is one of several Indiana county seats along the Lincoln Highway's Indiana route. Many communities have marked the highway's path with commemorative road signs, marking the way for the interested traveler.

Kosciusko
COUNTY

HISTORIC LINCOLN

1928 Route

Zale Drugs

1775 E. Center Street
Warsaw
(574) 267-7356

Zale Drugs has been serving its customers' needs – both pharmaceutical and gastronomic – since 1971.

The homey luncheonette is a big draw, store manager Lloyd Shroyer says. "During the week, it's packed in here at lunch. From 11 to 1, it's standing room only."

Daily specials are planned several weeks ahead by chef Betsy Bayne, but you can count on a homemade noodle dish every Wednesday. About 100 people receive the specials via email as they change every two weeks. Among the luncheonette's best sellers are the chili, the vegetable soup, the burgers, the breaded cheeseburger, the tenderloin and the homemade pies.

Jim Weaver, Jeanne White and Jeanne Colder settle in at Zale Drug's lunch counter, where the weekday noontime traffic is nearly constant. (Brian Tombaugh)

3-IN-1 CHICKEN

(courtesy of chef Betsy Bayne)

2 chickens
6 stalks of celery, diced
1 medium onion, diced
2 loaves of bread, torn in small pieces

6 eggs
Pepper
½ Tbsp. sage

Boil chicken (keep broth). Take skin and bones from chicken and tear meat into small pieces; keep in small amount of broth. Simmer celery and onions until tender. Mix bread, eggs, celery, onions, pepper and sage with enough broth to make soupy. Put in 10 x 15 pan and bake at 350 degrees for 1½ hours. Thicken remaining broth for gravy. When dressing is done, top with chicken. Serve with mashed potatoes and gravy.

(Brian Tombaugh)

Food is served at a counter that encompasses the back wall of the store and is decorated with Coca-Cola-themed items. The serving area has been expanded to include four dining tables already set with straws, toothpicks and hand sanitizer.

"Something we're pretty big on is local businesses," Lloyd says. Many of the luncheonette's ingredients are supplied by nearby Pierceton Foods.

The local feel also dominates the pharmacy, where store owner Becky Shroyer is behind the counter. The Butler University graduate specializes in compounding – taking the raw components of a medicine and combining them into forms and strengths to match each patient's needs. Since 2003, Becky also has focused on hormone consultation for female customers; she develops bioidentical hormones to bolster a woman's health. Patients can buy specially made home remedies as well, from cough syrup to suppositories to bedsore cream.

Even the family pets receive specialized treatment at Zale. "We work with vets to turn medicines into treats," Lloyd says.

The Shroyers bought the drugstore from pharmacist Gene Zale, who had purchased Judd Drugs to start his own business. Zale continued to work part time at the pharmacy until 2010.

Chinworth Bridge
Warsaw

Heading west out of Warsaw on old U.S. 30, at the intersection with County Road 350, a small park featuring a bright red bridge and a Lincoln Highway kiosk will catch your eye. This is the Chinworth Bridge, a National Register of Historic Places site.

The 138-foot Pratt through truss bridge spanning the Tippecanoe River was built in 1897 by the Bellefontaine (Ohio) Bridge & Iron Company. The contract for $2,520 ($18 per linear foot) was let in April; the bridge was completed in August.

Chinworth Bridge (named after property owner Robert Chinworth) was studied as a possibility for the 1928 route of the Lincoln Highway. But the surveyors and engineers "decided to bypass it because the structure was too light and too narrow for motor vehicular traffic. Also, the bridge sat at right angles to traffic at both ends if (the Lincoln Highway) crossed it," according to the nomination form.

The bridge closed to all but pedestrian traffic in 1975; it received its new coat of paint in 1992.

The 1995 book *Kosciusko County: A Pictorial History* notes the bridge also was known as the Orien Bridge in reference to a nearby village; the National Register form refers to "Orion."

Both images: A 1996 National Register nomination form describes the Chinworth Bridge site as "originally a ford where teams and wagons could cross safely in the shallow water." (Brian Tombaugh)

Etna Green

As the bypassed route makes its way farther west out of Warsaw, it passes through a series of communities that once bustled. Though they no longer see the activity they saw when the Lincoln Highway was Main Street, each has retained its own charm. The first of these is Etna Green.

Towering over the town is the Etna Elevator, a fixture for more than 135 years. The building on-site today was put up in 1914-15 following a fire that destroyed the original structure on September 1, 1914. The elevator is run by Lyle (George) Faulkner II with the assistance of his daughters and son-in-law. Lyle's wife runs the Nappanee Grain Elevator (Lyle is a Nappanee-area native). The family bought Etna Elevator for $5,000 in 2000 and before opening cleared out waist-deep piles of corn and soybeans that had been left rotting in the basement.

Remembrance Park offers another tie to Etna Green's past. Its focal point is the restored, elevated bandstand, an octagonal beadboard structure that sits atop a four-post base. The bandstand, which originally was located on a downtown corner, had been sold to a local landowner for use as a storage shed. A total of $178,000 was raised to repurchase and restore the bandstand so it could be put on display at the park. Other highlights include brick-paved walkways and a drinking fountain fed from a well. On the wall of the building that forms the park's southern border is a mural by local artist Robert A. Hudson. Hudson worked his signature in via a sign painted into the mural depicting a rural scene featuring a waterfall, horses grazing in a pasture ringed by a stone wall, and a white church with a cemetery.

A few blocks farther south on South Walnut Street is the Etna Green Museum, which opened in 2009. In addition to the displays inside, museum pieces include a refurbished 1920 Minneapolis, Northfield and Southern Railway caboose (which Santa Claus visits annually), and the cornerstone and bell from the 1914 Etna Township High School. (The school ceased to exist in 1963, when it merged with Bourbon and Tippecanoe schools to form the Triton district.)

Among the town's dining and drinking options is the Etna Green Cafe – which advertises "good home cooking" on its menu. The café has gone through several name changes through the years, from Cottage Lunch to the Honey Bee. A 2003 sesquicentennial history of Etna Green recalls the restaurant as "a great hangout for the town kids in the 1940s."

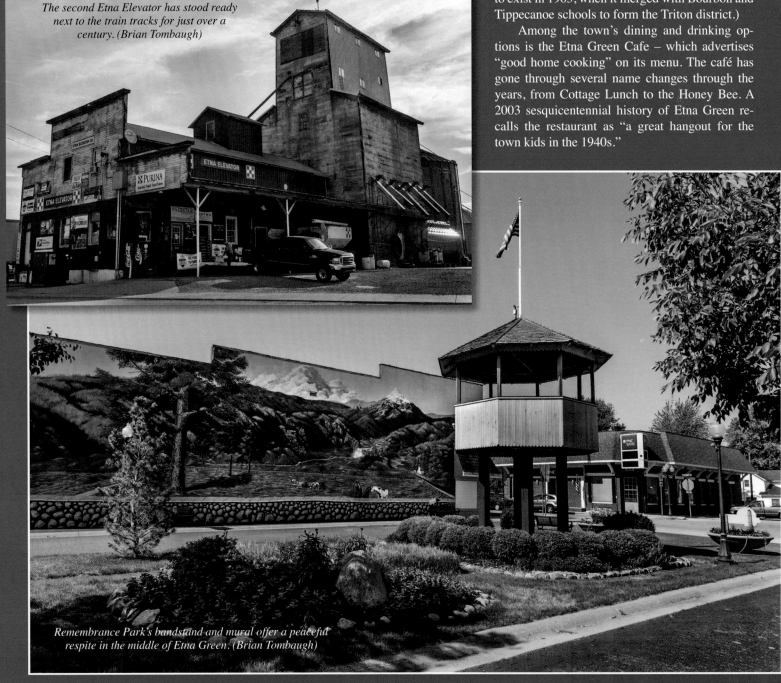

The second Etna Elevator has stood ready next to the train tracks for just over a century. (Brian Tombaugh)

Remembrance Park's bandstand and mural offer a peaceful respite in the middle of Etna Green. (Brian Tombaugh)

(Brian Tombaugh)

Marshall County is one of two places in Indiana where the Lincoln and Dixie highways intersect (the other is in South Bend). A telephone pole with an original red-white-and-blue Lincoln Highway marker, such as this one west of downtown Plymouth, is a rare find, indeed. (A sliver of the highway cuts through Starke County to the west of Marshall County.)

Marshall & Starke

COUNTIES

Both images: The top floor of this three-story building was once a ballroom where Bourbon's town band practiced. The town's Rainbow Girls also met in the ballroom and held their formal dances there. (Brian Tombaugh; courtesy Marshall County Historical Society)

The Great Apple
102 N. Main Street
Bourbon

The building that houses Bourbon's The Great Apple restaurant – at the northeast corner of the Lincoln Highway and Indiana 331 – "has been a lot of different things in its lifetime," says Great Apple manager Sherrie Leeper. She says there have been two or three grocery stores, a theater and an undertaker's business at the site, plus the former three-lane bowling alley that is now The Great Apple's side dining room. "But mostly, it's been a restaurant." As long ago as 1928, it was known as the Federal Lunch.

Lemler Locker

108 S. Main Street
Bourbon

As you look around the Lemler Locker, you notice the memorabilia, which has been accumulating since the family opened the meat shop in 1947. It's only a fraction of the Bourbon memorabilia Larry Lemler has accumulated throughout his life.

Plaques showing the cuts of beef and pork hang on the wall, and a set of sleigh bells once worn by livestock frames the entranceway. Lemler is noted especially for its seasoned sausage. It also carries a line of cured and smoked meats as well as some specialty products, in addition to its beef and pork cuts. Larry and son Jeff, a co-owner, will process your butchered cattle or hog.

Larry – whose decision to retire in the spring of 2016 will result in the locker's closure – is apt to pull out a photo album or an old menu as the conversation sparks a memory.

BEEF BRISKET
(courtesy of the Lemler family)

1 bottle Heinz chili sauce
1 package of Lipton onion soup mix
1 can of regular Coca-Cola
2 ½ lb. boneless brisket, trimmed close

Mix chili sauce with soup mix. Add Coca-Cola. Stir together carefully. Put brisket on durable foil big enough to fully cover. Pour mixture over meat and cover tightly. Bake at 300 degrees for five hours.

Sharon, Larry, Jeff and Barb Lemler are a storehouse of knowledge about Bourbon history – as well as meat. (Brian Tombaugh)

Sit Park
Bourbon

Sit Park, at the northwest corner of the old Lincoln Highway and Indiana 331, is designed for just what its name implies. The area around the centerpiece white gazebo is meticulously landscaped; the setting invites passers-by to stop and sit awhile. You can watch the traffic pass, gaze on the Ten Commandments monument or examine what Bourbonites call the symbol of their community – the stone Old Town Pump. The memorial was originally erected in 1929 in remembrance of the wooden pump that served the town in an earlier age.

(Brian Tombaugh)

OUT OF THE PAST

A&W Root Beer Stand
Bourbon

Bourbon's A&W Root Beer stand, like so many others across America, was known for its curbside ordering and carhops serving food to hungry drivers and passengers.

(Courtesy Larry Lemler)

OUT OF THE PAST

Berkey's Hamburgers
Bourbon

Berkey's Hamburgers was a popular postgame hangout for teenagers growing up in and around Bourbon.

(Courtesy Larry Lemler)

Mail Pouch Barn

Mail Pouch-painted barns were once a common site on highways across America. This one east of Plymouth is the lone remaining such building on Indiana's Lincoln Highway routes. Judy McCullough, whose family since 1890 has farmed the land on which the building sits, says it "is in sad shape. We put a metal roof on it but are not certain how to save the side walls. ... We had the sign repainted a number of years ago, but it is fading quite a bit at this time. We have been advised both ways – repaint to restore it; don't repaint, it will lose authenticity." Mail Pouch stopped paying painters to maintain the white, black and yellow signs ("Chew Mail Pouch Tobacco. Treat Yourself to the Best") in 1969.

(Brian Tombaugh)

Marshall County Infirmary
10924 Lincoln Highway
Plymouth

About 3 miles east of Plymouth sits an imposing brick-and-limestone building with a signature arched, recessed entryway. The Shady Rest Home assisted-living facility carries on the building's history of caring for Marshall County's most in-need residents.

The Romanesque Revival infirmary was completed in 1895 at a cost of $79,547.50, according to a 2000 National Register of Historic Places nomination form (status was granted the same year). The building was executed by the prominent Fort Wayne architectural firm of Wing & Mahurin (a near-duplicate of the Marshall County building can be found in Indiana's Sullivan County).

The façade visible to those passing on the Lincoln Highway was the site superintendent's quarters. Behind that building sat a dormitory – demolished and replaced in 1978 – as well as a kitchen and dining facility. Among the ornate touches in the superintendent's quarters are marble fireplaces and herringbone-brick floors in the basement. Outside, orchards of shade and fruit trees planted at the time of construction more than 100 years ago lend the site its current name – Shady Rest.

Also on the grounds is the Shady Rest Barn, which was renovated in 2003. An earthen embankment leads to the main level of the basement-style barn, which is topped by an aluminum replica cupola.

To the east of the Marshall County Infirmary sits the meticulously restored Shady Rest Barn, which is available to tour and to rent for events. (Brian Tombaugh)

Above: Originally the Marshall County rest home, the building is still in use today as a residence for those in need. (Brian Tombaugh)

OUT OF THE PAST

Schori's Restaurant
314 E. Jefferson Street
Plymouth

Robert and Barbara Schori found success as restaurateurs on the Lincoln Highway stretch from Warsaw to Plymouth. They opened their first restaurant in Etna Green and moved west through Bourbon. In 1958, the Schoris bought Howell's Chicken in the Rough in Plymouth and turned it into their namesake restaurant.

Around the same time, the Schoris became acquainted with Col. Harland Sanders, who had begun traveling to enlist franchisees for his fast-growing chain of Kentucky Fried Chicken restaurants. The couple signed on and for 30 years were franchisees who managed five locations. (During a similar trip to Fort Wayne,

The site of Schori's Restaurant is now home to Plymouth's Boys and Girls Club. (Courtesy Russell Rein)

Sanders made the acquaintance of Dave Thomas, who was later to emulate the KFC business model with his Wendy's Hamburgers chain.)

OUT OF THE PAST

Candy Bungalow
611 E. Jefferson Street
Plymouth

Plymouth's Candy Bungalow, on the town's eastern Lincoln Highway edge, offered patrons the "finest homemade candies."

(Courtesy Marshall County Historical Society)

Crossroads Center / Marshall County Historical Society

123 N. Michigan Street
Plymouth
(574) 936-2306

In 2002, the Marshall County Historical Society bought the two buildings immediately to its south (121 and 119 West Michigan). Those buildings date from as early as the 1890s, and at various times in their history, they have housed a saloon, a cigar store, a bakery, a lunch stand and an attorney's office. They since have been joined into a three-story structure that details the county's history and development.

Plymouth's location at the intersection of U.S. 30 and U.S. 31 places it at the crossroads of the nation's first transcontinental road and the first road connecting the Ohio Valley to Lake Michigan. That central location also makes the Crossroads Center the ideal repository for Indiana's Lincoln Highway history.

Below: The converted-storefront façade of the Marshall County Museum offers passersby a glimpse of the treasures that await inside. (Brian Tombaugh)

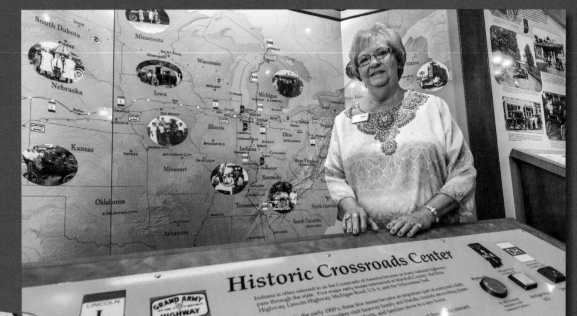

Above: Museum executive director Linda Rippy shows off the display that explains the county's designation as the "crossroads center." Michigan Road – plus the Dixie and Grand Army of the Republic highways – join the Lincoln Highway (in lights on the map) in crisscrossing Marshall County. (Brian Tombaugh)

HOT CROSSROADS BUNS

(adapted 1927 recipe courtesy of Linda Rippy, Marshall County Historical Society)

1¾ cups bread flour	¼ cup Mazola oil
¼ cup cornstarch	1 Tbsp. Karo, Red Label
½ tsp. salt	1 egg, beaten lightly
1 Tbsp. baking powder	¾ cup milk

Sift together the dry ingredients. Stir in the Mazola, Karo, egg and milk. Transfer to a floured board and pat to one-fourth-inch thickness. Cut in rounds, crease each to form a hinge, brush with a little Mazola and fold into pocket shape. Transfer to a pan oiled with Mazola and bake for twenty to twenty-five minutes in a hot oven (375 to 400 degrees).

OUT OF THE PAST

The Barrel
Plymouth

"The Barrel" originated in Plymouth as Roy's Cider Barrel – it was built by Leroy Williams – sometime around 1931 on West Jefferson Street along what was then the southern edge of the city. The featured drink was supplied courtesy of a nearby cider mill. An attached structure was added in the mid-1940s; the barrel portion was removed in 1962.

Both images:
(Courtesy Marshall County Historical Society)

Mobil Gas Station

1101 W. Jefferson Street
Plymouth

Heading west out of downtown Plymouth, keep an eye out on the left-hand side of the road – where Barney Fife will be keeping an eye out for you. The Barney dummy sits in a vintage police cruiser outside a restored Mobil gas station.

Calvin Bailey, owner of Bailey's Furniture Store, undertook the task of sprucing up the site. Mobil's trademark Pegasus logo soars over the white, red-trimmed building. Globe-topped pumps flanked by period-appropriate lamps stand out front. A 1960 city directory identifies the business as Ludwig's Oklahoma Service Station; later in the 1960s, it became Ludwig's Enco Service Station. A sign on the building advertising gasoline for 29 cents a gallon and a telephone booth around the side add to the 1960s feel.

(Brian Tombaugh)

(Brian Tombaugh)

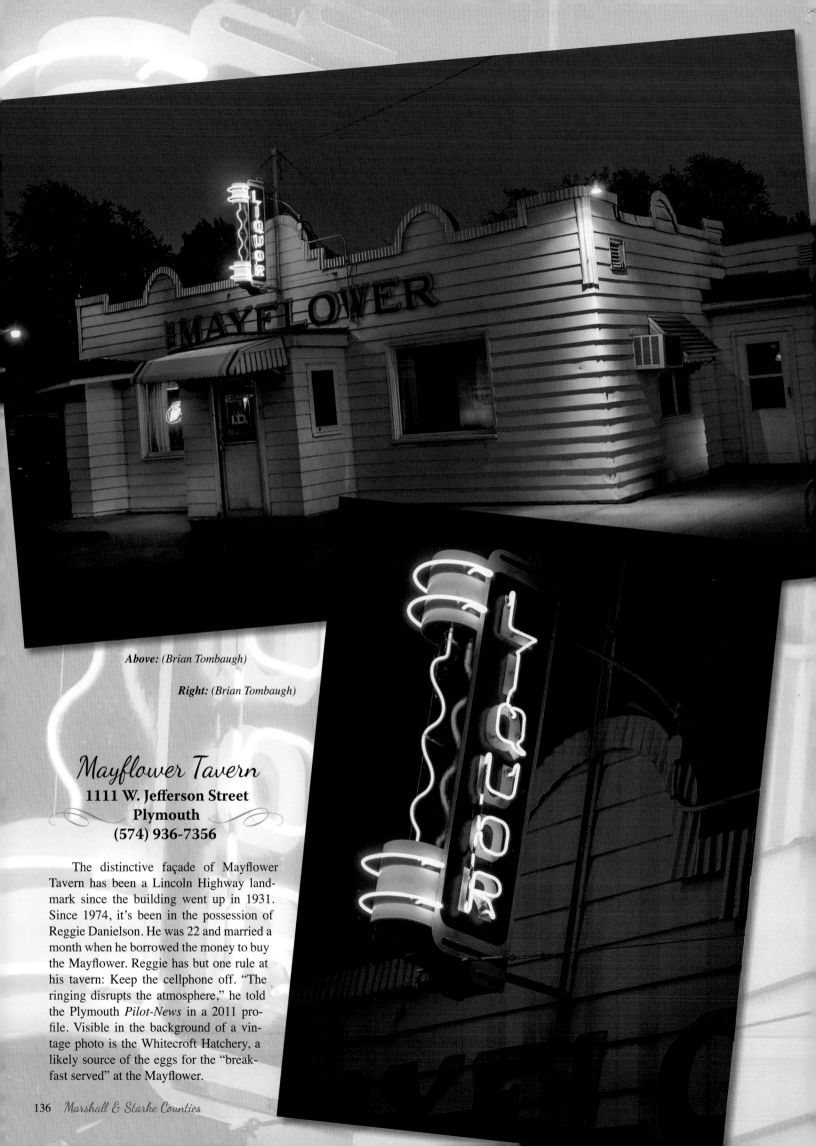

Above: (Brian Tombaugh)

Right: (Brian Tombaugh)

Mayflower Tavern
1111 W. Jefferson Street
Plymouth
(574) 936-7356

The distinctive façade of Mayflower Tavern has been a Lincoln Highway landmark since the building went up in 1931. Since 1974, it's been in the possession of Reggie Danielson. He was 22 and married a month when he borrowed the money to buy the Mayflower. Reggie has but one rule at his tavern: Keep the cellphone off. "The ringing disrupts the atmosphere," he told the Plymouth *Pilot-News* in a 2011 profile. Visible in the background of a vintage photo is the Whitecroft Hatchery, a likely source of the eggs for the "breakfast served" at the Mayflower.

OUT OF THE PAST

Mrs. Bennett's Railside Inn
Grovertown

Carl and Rose Bennett's 1946 cross-country trip ended abruptly in Grovertown, Indiana. "They were on their way to California looking for work when they heard this small restaurant was for sale," recalls daughter Lou Ann (Bennett) Clemens in a reminiscence for the Marshall County Historical Society. "All of our (belongings) were in the car

dad was driving, and we lived in one of the cabins for a year until they could afford to build a small house for us to live in."

A quarter-chicken dinner at Bennett's cost $1.25; $2.25 got you a half chicken with all the trimmings. Turkey dinners also were available on Sundays.

As the business took off, the Bennetts expanded.

"They (built) a new restaurant that would seat 100 people," Lou Ann says. "Still, on Sundays, I can remember people waiting outside for a table to come empty so they could come in and eat."

Bennett's was popular among families visiting sons at the nearby Culver Military Academy; it gained a wider reputation, as well.

"I can remember the day the helicopter landed," says Lou Ann. "The people (were) from the state of Washington and were visiting friends in Fort Wayne, and the friends from Fort Wayne told them about the restaurant."

As the four-lane U.S. 30 supplanted the Lincoln Highway, business dwindled. The Bennetts retired in 1962.

Smoker Farm

9295 W. U.S. Highway 30
Wanatah

Smoker Farm is an easily recognizable Lincoln Highway landmark, especially at harvest time. That's when Greg and Debbie Smoker's children earn their college money.

They started with a small patch that yielded 25 pumpkins. These days, you can get a pumpkin from their large selection for anywhere from $1 to $35, depending on your needs. Gourds and specialty treats such as strawberry popcorn are available, as well. Corn shocks and a miniature corn maze for the children add to the festive ambiance.

The 1,400-acre farm produces plenty more, including wheat, hay, corn and soybeans, as well as cattle. The farm's large barn has loomed over the Lincoln Highway since 1936. At that time, only the southern two lanes of the four-lane U.S. 30 ran past the family's front door.

PIT BARBEQUE

(courtesy of Jacob Smoker)

Use hard wood, no pine, elm or hedge. Body wood is best. It takes about three holes full of wood to burn into charcoal. Average time to start is about six hours before to put meat in (which should be given 12 hours in the pit). Charcoal should be within 12-15 inches from the top of the pit. Cover charcoal with ¾ inch of dirt. Put wrapped meat on dirt and cover quickly. Use steel posts or pipe and cover with metal roofing. Finally, cover it with 9 inches of dirt so it is airtight. Don't open for 12 hours.

The meat should be made into 15- to 22-pound roasts. They should not be over 5 inches thick and a foot long. The meat should be seasoned several hours before wrapping. Do it while the wood is burning. To season, mix 1 ounce garlic powder with 5 pounds kosher salt. Rub in meat (at least 3 pounds to every 100 pounds of meat).

When you open the pit, the meat will look red like it did when put in. But when it is out and air hits it, it will turn grey and tender. To wrap meat, tie in cheesecloth. Wrap with one thickness of paper, using an envelope fold with all edges turned up so no juice can run out. Then wrap it with one thickness of wet burlap. It is ready to lay on the fire. Try to keep pieces from touching the edges or each other.

Supplies needed: Meat, long-handle fire tools, several dirt shovels, wood, steel posts and metal roofing to cover pit, salt and garlic powder, cheesecloth, burlap, parchment paper, buckets for salt and water, tub to soak burlap, freezer tape, knives, gloves, towels and aprons, 10-16 penny nails to pin burlap on, tables to work on and plastic to cover tables. Pit should be 8 feet long, 40 inches wide, and 36 to 40 inches deep.

Both images: In the fall, you'd be forgiven for thinking that the Smoker Farm is primarily a pumpkin patch. But the family produces much more on its 1,400 acres. (Brian Tombaugh)

THE SMOKER FARM
EST. 1944
WANATAH, IND.

MUMS

3.00

2.50

PUMPKINS
KIDS MAZE
THRU BARN

Wanatah

This town of 1,000 people is a quick gas/rest stop for many U.S. 30 travelers. But those who take the time to stop and explore are richly rewarded.

A restored Monon Railroad caboose, circa 1888, houses train-related memorabilia and other Wanatah historical artifacts. And a plaque memorializes the spot where President Abraham Lincoln's funeral train passed on May 1, 1865, during its journey from Washington, D.C., to Springfield, Illinois. (A similar plaque can be found in Westville.)

A park also on-site, dedicated in honor of the nation's bicentennial in 1976, is a tribute to William F. Hunt. A piece of preserved printing press salutes the longtime publisher of the *Wanatah Mirror* weekly newspaper. A stroll across a metal truss footbridge carries you to the caboose museum.

Looking south, the bed of the long-gone railway that carried President Lincoln home is evident nearly 150 years later. The site received a recent upgrade, including a new sign. (Brian Tombaugh)

(Brian Tombaugh)

Index

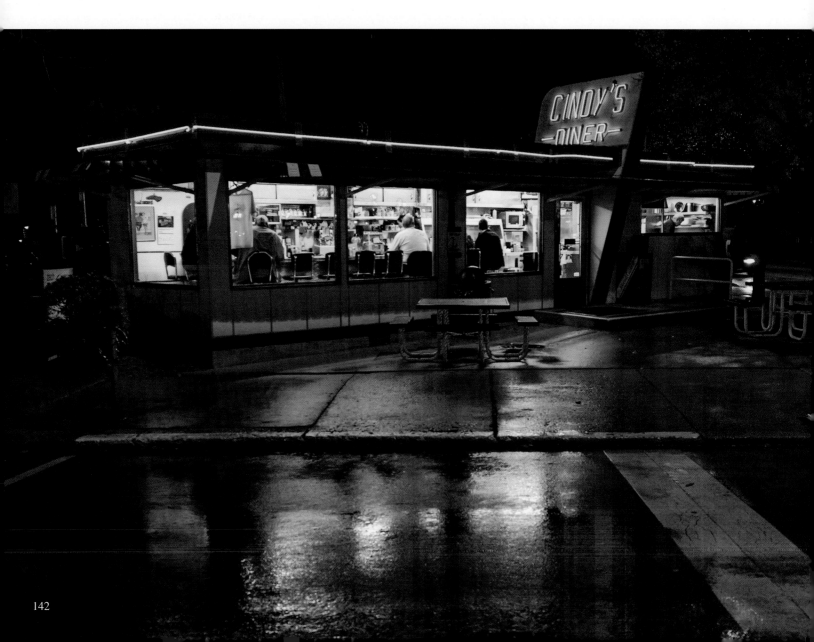

Recipe Index